MW00325000

How to Start a Daycare/Preschool as a Mission:

Your Most Important Mission Can Pay for Itself

Sharon Sarles, M.Div., M.A.

Copyright © 2018 Sharon Sarles

All rights reserved.

ISBN-10: 0965777022

ISBN-13: 978-0965777025 (Organizational Strategies)

:

DEDICATION

To all the teachers who nurtured me.

CONTENTS

1   What is YOUR Most Important Mission?   3
    Evangelism, Charity, or Academic Achievement?
    Why a CDC is a priority.
    CDC, After-school Center or School?

2   Answers to Important Questions   21

    Liability, Facilities, Shared Space, Inconvenience, Expense, Cultural
    Gaps, Spanking

3   Count the Cost and Also Count the Return   32

4   Discover and Plan   38

    Space and plumbing, Market Assessment, Regulations, Business Plan

5   Organize and Implement   47

    Organize to Avoid Problems, Checklist of Steps

6   Buy Equipment Frugally and Share Space Happily   55

7   Heart of Education -- Curricula and Staff   62

8   Heart of Hearts: Chapel – Our Most Important Hour   70

9   Bringing in Money and Spreading it Around   74

10 Last Words   81

    Warnings, Offers, and Decisions

ACKNOWLEDGMENTS

Many thanks to Pamela den Ouden for editing help.
All the mistakes are mine.

About the cover picture: The two children are happy because they have been cared for and are on a way to a successful life, showing forth the glory of God. Sometimes we have a picture with an inset of an unhappy teen. He is unhappy because he doesn't feel cared for, doesn't have much purpose in life, and feel trapped. We hope we can empower you to care for children in such a way that they have good choices, become successful, and show forth the love of God.

1 WHAT IS **YOUR** MOST IMPORTANT MISSION?

What is your most important mission? Is it evangelism? Is it discipleship? Is it membership recruitment? Is it social outreach, service, practical works of charity? Is it being a witness? Is it modeling God's love? Pastors and boards have various angles on what their most important task is. I will here outline a mission that is related to each and everyone of these questions, making it possibly the most important step in missions today.

Write *your* overall
mission:_____

Related to all of these questions is an overlooked sector of society.

They need evangelizing.

They need discipleship and formation.

Many of them need charity.

They and their families might become church members.

They are innocent.

Most of American children do not have adequate parenting.

Group rearing will determine their character.

This makes this mission even more important.

If Evangelism Is Your Most Important Mission

If evangelism is your most important mission, then isn't it most important to evangelize first the children of your own families and then the children of your own neighborhood, then those of churches wherever in the world you partner with other churches? Of course, let's go to the world, but the children closest to us, isn't that like starting in Jerusalem?

We are used to thinking of children being taken care of, churched, and evangelized as a matter of course of the church's doing its usual thing. However, today, younger generations are less likely to be "churched" (Barna, 2014). Interestingly for our purposes, this same article suggests that an increasing number would like to access church first in some other way than Sunday services. Certainly our public education system, very much unlike the American education of earlier times, will not teach them any religion. Further, there will probably not be any character development training. They may, in fact, be taught an anti-Christian bias. Furthermore, they may even be trained in thinking that there are no deadlines and no possible failure! They may come to believe that rewards and encouragements are hollow and manipulative! In short, in our public education system, training for the work force itself is in question and thorough discipleship is nonexistent for nearly all of our children. Unless something changes.

Many churches have historically seen it as their duty to promote either their own private schools or the public schools in general. However, both missions are increasingly being forgotten. May the tribe increase that can turn around the public school system for good. But such a huge job will clearly take longer than any given child has to wait. Every child needs education now and revamping the public school system will take more than 20 years, if it is even possible. So let's turn toward what may be done for children alive and in your neighborhood today.

The fact is that every decade fewer church affiliated child development centers are being started, according to the state records in Texas (http://www.dfps.state.tx.us/Child_Care/). It seems to me that, similarly, also fewer private church affiliated schools are being established. There are many reasons for this. Firstly, more of the population is in non-denominational and lower socio-economic status churches. It was always those higher SES denominations that invested in education. (Of course, any who invest in education tend become higher SES than they were.) Further, many churches that once had schools now promote homeschooling. Of course, I applaud the movement to support home education. Undeniably, it has had a great result. Yet, the mission toward unchurched, the poor, or single parent families has been overlooked. While there is a great deal more support for homeschoolers than in the past, not everyone can homeschool and not everyone is successful. More resource centers and co-ops may be needed. However, there is certainly also a need for more private school options.

The need is the greatest at the preschool level for many reasons, but especially since character is formed before age seven. Further more, a great deal of brain happens before a child reaches seven. No wonder the government wants to increase preschool education.

About one-third of our children are born and/or reared without a father in the home (CDC 2017, NCF 2017, US Census Bureau 2016). Reports of the percentage of children who will be without a father in the home at some time in their life *for any reason* are certainly about half and estimates range up to 73% for some categories. (US Census 2013, Pew 2015, Politifact 2013)., Children-and-Divorce.com 2017, Jacobson 2013). My book, *The Government is not a Village* covers the worsening of such statistics from the 1990s to recent times in more detail.

If such a great proportion of our nation's children are at some time in a single parent household, there is a great need for child chare and early childhood education. Single parents typically have to work. Even two parent households often find themselves both working. Most young grandmothers also must work. Most children, then, are being reared in daycares. The good ones are few. None replace a good mother. I will admit that the quality is coming up in many regards, but character development, let alone spiritual formation, is not being addressed.

What is your observation? Are children generally well formed in terms of character? Educational initiative? Brain development? General health and good physiology?

It has seemed that those schools and preschools that are the best academically are also the best at pushing non-traditional values. From graduate school to Common Core, a more leftist, more socially experimental value set is what is valued. This is true in early childhood education also. For instance, I was told, while in a training session for directors of Association for the Education of Young Children (AEYC) run by someone employed full time on government money to teach and mentor directors, that every classroom must have at least one book introducing homosexuality and every classroom must have at least one lesson on it. Of course, I assume they meant lessons that were developmentally appropriate: for example, Johnny has two mothers, so let's not be mean to Johnny. In fact, I could not find this dictum in the AEYC published rules but it was taught, by the local authority, who was teaching nervous directors how to get re-accredited. It is in some other standards, and I suspect it soon will be in all.

While this is just one issue, it is illustrative, but even setting aside controversies, when was the last time you heard lessons on honesty, diligence, and repentance? In fact, I hear teachers complaining about what they call the "old kiss and make-up" method. They feel this somehow harms children's authenticity.

There is a great gulf between generations on being willing to accept character formation lessons. There is an ocean of *difference between value sets.*

If you want something done correctly, you must do it yourself. Children are being evangelized into a value set, but are these values Christian? American? When these children grow up and hear the gospel, will it sound like truth and good to them? Or will they have been so trained that they know automatically that Christianity is something they should avoid as detrimental? That traditional values are nothing but bigotry and ignorance? That capitalism is merely greed always, or that diligence and manners are silly old-fashioned conceits? Preschools, schools, and after-school ministries are the most important evangelism mission in our world today.

If Charitable Mission is Your Aim

Granted, for some, evangelism is not the primary concern, or if it is, it is mediated through concern for social welfare. Some may wish to evangelize through serving. In other congregations, it may be felt that evangelism is being covered and what they need now is a way to serve charitably. Please allow me to draw your attention to the importance of child development centers as the highest priority for domestic charitable mission.

Firstly, it is well known that those under 18 are the poorest category of Americans (NCCP 2017). Those under 5 would be much more likely to be in a household under the poverty line (Yang 2017). No, we are not arriving at this statistic based on the fact that children fail to earn money! It is just that *household income* is related to youth of parents, family structure, and fertility rate. It is people who are younger and poorer themselves who have more children. Part of this dynamic is unavoidable: one must make babies before one can reach the highest wage. Babies come to young people and older people have reached the zenith of their career. On the other hand, part of this dynamic is causative: young people who have babies when they are very young tend to make a great deal less money than those who put off childbearing in favor or education and career development. Similarly, of course, families who have one wage earner because the other adult stays home to parent has less income. However, there is still the fact that many children are being born into situations where the parents are too young and too poor to adequately provide for their children. There is also the fact of differential fertility, meaning poorer Americans have more children than do richer ones. Certainly, young unwed mothers tend to have lower incomes than most other families.

The point is that if you want to help the poor, you can do so best by helping children. Similarly, if you want to find the *deserving* poor, look to children, because obviously they are not at fault for their poverty. Further, if you want to reverse generational poverty, educate children.

Please notice that relatively little attention is paid to children. Increasingly, families are turning their attention to survival and thus toward working. The grandmothers who once took up childcare duties are themselves working, often toward their own survival. Many accounts of child abuse and sexual abuse come from family members placing their children with questionable relatives because they feel they have no other choice. Then notice too, that increasingly group childcare is taken over by large corporations, who make decisions based primarily on accounting principles. Finally, as churches age, they too tend to turn their focus away from children, toward their mature donors.

Lastly, government run daycares are the worst of the industry: the standards and expectations are the lowest, and the results compared to the children remaining in a poverty stricken situation without education during those years evaporates by they time they are twelve (Lips & Mulhausen, 2010, OPRE 2010 , US Dept HHS 2010). We do have a large amount of money going to government funded daycare, but 1) the results are the poor, and extremely poor compared to church affiliated centers, 2) the improvement compared to no educational intervention, while significant at first, diminishes to negligible by 6th grade at least, and 3) given the government's dire financial straits, it is unlikely to increase. Indeed, given current government policies, any character formation attempted and any academics undertaken may well be in the wrong direction. Further, there is no way to improve the outcome through regulation. Regulations are so tight now that private owners are screaming and leaving the field.

At the same time, the statistics of single-parent households correlate with low academic achievement, crime, and health problems Allen & Daley 2007, Hymowitz 2012, MacLanahan, Tach, and Schneider 2013). Hillary Clinton was correct when she cited many social problems that go along with poverty as correlates of the problems of educating children in her 1990s book, *It Takes a Village*. Unfortunately, all those statistics have gotten significantly worse. For more on this, see my book, *The Government is not a Village* www.thegovernmentisnotavillage.com.

One statistic that Clinton didn't even mention was the rate of children who are traumatized by sex trafficking. Of course there were some children who were sex trafficked in the 1990s, but the amount and rate today seems to be great deal higher. I seriously doubt that this was as large a problem always, and we merely got smarter about finding it. Rather, I think our culture has been vastly sexualized by both the reduction in Christianity and the increase in porn. We are now just realizing the increase in this horrific problem. Traditionally problems of trauma from sex trafficking and sexual exploitation were thought to be few, temporary, and caused by poverty. The problems today are more widespread, and the increase is much greater than the increase in the rate of poverty. It is clear that many subsequent problems in life either stem from or were exacerbated by sexual trauma. One is too many. And we have an explosion.

Furthermore, it is well established that children form their basic personality and worldview before they are seven. They establish much of their cognitive ability in these tender years, as well. Trauma damages the brain as well as inducing psychological problems. In the first years of school, views of authorities, learning, and achievement are established. Clearly then, providing good care, let alone academically enriching care, **is not only an important charitable service but will obviate the need for other kinds of charitable service later.** It will serve not only the child and its family now, but society going forward.

We have seen some data that reflects that supporting the family structure is a cost effective way to reduce such sad statistics as have been mentioned such as poor academic achievement, criminal victimization, sexual exploitation, poor self concept, and poverty (Allen 2007, MacLanhan et. al. 2013). For this reason, during the George W. Bush administration marriages were being promoted. While I had reservations about coercing the establishment of marriage between young people who were not otherwise considering it simply because of a pregnancy, the policy does illustrate an application to the finding that, overall, having 2 adults in the household reduced a variety of problems. Often when a family is pressed considerably by poverty, the fathers leave in search of work but find other situations, or stay intermittently, allowing the mother to collect higher government aid. Might the feeling of being able to have the children taken care of encourage the father to stay around? Alternatively, when a mother can put her child into good, consistent care, she is better able to be a good, consistent employee. If a two parent family would benefit from such support, clearly, a one parent family would benefit as well. Providing a family with good childcare options is a way to support any fragile family.

 Research establishes that congregationally affiliated schools result in better academic outcomes, *even controlling for amount of household income*. Researchers believe this is because all the congregations studied (Christian and Jewish) taught values that result in better grades (Jeynes 2003). Furthermore, only a church can provide the extended support for the parents emotionally, morally, and spiritually, beyond the hours of childcare. Only a church can provide the support needed AND the guidance on how to avoid the need later. A government program, by contrast, normalizes the need and so increases its likelihood through society and time. The public school system has failed, yet funding and its reach ever increases. It is likely that a president like Hillary Clinton would vastly expand pre-school education in public school, insuring increasing problems. Please see my book, *The Government is not a Village, www.thegovernmentisnotavillage.com..*

So for all the increasingly bad statistics for children in America and for all the well established findings that enrichment in younger life helps brain and character development, having a child development center should rate as the most effective and thus most necessary charitable project.

If Improvement Of Academic Achievement

Some groups may feel that both evangelism and charity are covered in their situation, and that their prime concern is finding a way to improve academic performance. Clearly, developing a school with higher standards or more access is the way to provide academic achievement. Perhaps a congregation with modest means might question their ability to accomplish this task. There is robust research that suggests that congregational affiliated schools produced much better academic results, even controlling for family income or even money spent in the school! For a meta-analysis of this research, see Jeynes' 2003 book, *Religion, Education and Academic Success.* Therefore yes, if higher academic performance is wanted, then starting a church affiliated or Judeo-Christian private school will almost necessarily yield a better result.

Certainly, we still have a problem with a low level of academic achievement in our public schools. Charlotte Iserbyt's work is a longitudinal study that suggests a long term intention to insure our poorer students, at least, fall behind in academic performance (Deliberate Dumbing 1999). Certainly, everyone knows that we have had calls for increased rigor and a contentious debate over methods. What is little known is that the testing itself tended to reduce academic expectations (Popham 2003). Generally educators agree that there are problems with a unitary assessment, with taking so much class time for testing, and with narrowing/reducing the curricula. Further, while administrators everywhere crow about incremental raising of statistics, and official charges of criminally manipulating scores have occurred, it is well established that U.S. academic performance remains very much behind other countries. Rereading the data, I notice that the call was to close the gap between high and low performers – not raise the average. At the same time, I heard reports of pervasively lowered morale for both students and teachers because we had mandated no limits to retesting and no deadlines. Since work was not rewarded and awarding failing grades was not an option, diligence plummeted. **Averages are up insignificantly**, but victory has been declared on aim. Indeed, in Texas, we have seen the bottom tier of students improved their *scores*, but **the upper tier went down.** This was thought to be due to the moving of funds from Gifted and Talented to remedial programs (Dana Center, Presentation to World Future Society, Austin, 2000) . Overall, the average has not changed much. Meanwhile, in other nations, it has risen (Bidwell, 2013). Thus The United States continues to be at the bottom of the list of developed countries and worse than many developing countries.

Making higher academic and behavioral requirements is clearly a worthy goal of such a project. Of course, providing higher academic achievement along with Christian values will profit society with better leadership. Clearly we need more and better leadership! Every time you wonder about a leader's integrity, think that you could contribute to a better crop of leaders for tomorrow.

Let me urge the consideration also of wider access as well. If the same handful who would be in a special enriched situation merely trade one for another, then an improved result may be somewhat limited. Only if children who would otherwise not have access to a better school, can now be in one, only then has society been helped. The good news is that this can rather readily be accomplished because better results do not depend as much on increased monies as on congregational affiliation (Jeynes 2003, Coleman 1982, 1988).

One way of doing this is to either have a sliding fee scale for tuition, or charge tuition at a market rate and make scholarship slots available. This is almost always doable as other people make profit and congregationally affiliated school spend less on buildings. Further, just as you do for congregational planning, plan for growth of the school. Often providing just a few more seats is well within possibility.

It is also possible to have two or more tiers of scholarship support, so that poorer members of the congregation are helped before those outside. There are companies who will take the task of sifting through personal financial data off the hands of the school and preserve the privacy of the families.

Academic performance in real terms is stagnant or down even after calls for "increased rigor" (Bidwell 2013, DeSilver 2017, Popham 2003). The number of private corporate schools is up and congregationally affiliated schools is down. Statistics show private schools and especially congregationally affiliated schools outperform (Jeynes 2003). Therefore, there is a clear argument for a market need for private, religious schools.

Therefore Child Development Centers (aka "Daycares") Must Be The Priority Of Mission Focus

Therefore, whether your aim is evangelism, social mission, or improvement of academic performance, you need to begin a child development center (CDC) (or school or after-school center depending upon your circumstances.) Moreover, the pay-off for this mission is higher than any other endeavor. Nothing can so dramatically and rapidly :

- change the lives of so many permanently and rapidly
- improve the economy of the neighborhood, as it permits some parents to work
- change the region permanently by providing a cadre of Christian leaders in 15-20 years
- provide financial sustainability within a year and possible ongoing profit.

There are not enough CDCs in any state. Further, in Texas, where I see records, I can see that each decade fewer and fewer churches have applied for a CDC license. At the same time, a much greater market share of early childhood education is taken up by large corporations. This means that it can be not only done but done profitably. Although individuals may less often take up the challenge today, there is a clear place for churches to do so.

Further, the radical political left is also working to have public school take over early childhood education. I have heard it said explicitly that they wish to mold the hearts and minds of young children before they are warped by their parents' sense of morality. This suggests that notions of sexuality, high birth rate, educational policy, political policy and cultural outcomes correlate. It certainly illustrates convincingly that early childhood education is an important influencer of culture.

Please circle those arguments above for starting a CDC that are most resonant *with you.* Then list the most important below.

_____

_____

_____

_____

_____

Then write them here, in the language that is most understandable and meaningful to *your* congregation.

_____

_____

_____

_____

_____

What facts presented in this chapter were most surprising?

_____

_____

_____

What arguments were most persuasive?

_____

_____

_____

_____

_____

What language has your congregation used up until now relating to early childhood?

_____

_____

_____

What has your congregation conceived to be its core mission?

_____

_____

_____

What are the most important words they use to talk about this core mission and their core values?

_____

_____

_____

What words most inspire or excite or cause higher aspirations for your congregation?

_____

_____

_____

Please craft a message stating how a preschool mission is at the core of what your congregation wishes to be and/or to do.

_____

_____

_____

_____

_____

_____

_____

_____

_____

After-School Centers

Not all churches have the property for a CDC. They may still start an after-school program or school. Some churches may be located near a public elementary school. A few have some specialty focus that could especially minister to their community. Churches that are near elementary schools or that can provide transportation, especially if they have a particular expertise to offer, are in ideal situations to provide after-school care.

After-school care is much needed. The highest crime time in America is between 3 p.m. and 7 p.m., the time between school letting out and parents getting home (OJJDP). Further, children 12-17 are most likely to be victimized by non family members during this after-school hours (OJJDP). Further, those who are going home to screens are increasingly vulnerable to pornography and online sexual predators (Gross 2013) . Further, children who are latchkey children are now vulnerable to sex-trafficking. Many think that afterschool programs would save children from both being victims and victimizing (After School Alliance 2007, Pederson et. al., 1999, Youth.gov [2017]), even though government funded program have produced less-than-rosy results (Edweek 2017.)

To the extent that schools can not, should not, or are not teaching everything a child might profitably know, then after-school time may be devoted to those topics. One group of centers focuses on citizenship, another on sports, and still another on entrepreneurship. Of course some focus on religious education.

There are two types of after-school programs you might want to consider: one in the church or one in the school. An after-school center may be a stand-alone enterprise, or an addition to a CDC or a school. The requirements for an after-school center are less onerous but typically under the same jurisdiction as are CDCs. Centers housed in public schools typically need adhere to only the lesser requirements that state requires of their own public school. There may be a total exemption from regulation for a religious or single-focus program. Have your lawyer check state laws for you.

A church across the street from a school can easily allow children to walk over and then provide homework time, a snack, and some physical activities. Sometimes the church playground and building will be more comfortable than the school building. Certainly the curriculum could be different. There might be more patient adults. There might be some patient grandparent types.

In-church after-school programs can vary. First Lutheran in Portland Maine offers a traditional program of a child care center that include after school care of children who come from the elementary school across the street, perhaps to be with their younger siblings until a parent can retrieve them. Crossroads Church in Fayetteville NC offers afterschool care and transports the students from several elementary school. Hill Country Bible Church (in northwest Austin) once ran an activity center in the poorest district of Austin, complete with snack, Bible story lesson, and art projects. Children and youth would walk in. Another church in Round Rock provides a boxing gym with professional level but volunteer coaches. They then aspired to a full after-school program with transportation, and options to learn music and sound production.

Full plans for such an after-school center in a church building, complete with tutoring and physical activities are available. Consultations are also available, tailored to your congregation's need to strategically design for your community's specific needs (www.orgstrat.net). Making center and other services offered by the congregation strategic parts of an overall plan increases effectiveness of mission and stability of finances.

Because of the recent new bathroom nondiscrimination laws, many churches who ran CDCs are now considering schools as well. It would be great if many Christian schools considered opening a CDC also.

There are some examples of churches offering afterschool care on public school property. A campus ministry founded by the Methodists and the Presbyterians at The University of Texas started an after hours drop-in center for university students in a church near campus, and then expanded into a secular non-profit offering after-school care in elementary schools in the area. Later, a coalition of churches proposed starting after-school centers in all the remaining elementary schools in the city.

There are a some Christian groups that do offer Christian programs on public school property. There are at least two longstanding clubs that present Christ and Christian living on various elementary campuses and at least three that have traditionally specialized in high school. While many public schools might resist a congregation offering programs on school property, it is not hard to imagine Christians making a non-profits for character or skills development without sectarian doctrine. A non-profit has entered Boston schools in order to offer citizenship classes after hours – with great success. There have been business groups who have offered in-class lessons. One Rotarian group here has made repeated visits to a local Head Start. Thus, it is easy to imagine an organization offering civic, entrepreneurial, or technological classes after school in the school building. These might provide encouragement in providing examples of prominent community members who are of the same ethnicity. It might include character development lessons.

When neither a preschool nor an after-school program can be accommodated, still there are other possible supports to community education. Some church buildings that while not acceptable for a CDC, might house a small elementary school for its own members. Many churches can find a room for a library and a meeting for the local homeschool coalition. Nearly any could house a free English class for new immigrants. A few manage to mount a rather thorough adult vocational training center. Every church can do something in the way of contributing to education in the community. All of these are worthy projects; please consider them after considering the mission of the preschool.

I expect you now understand why starting a CDC, a school, or an after-school center is so very vital. Perhaps you have some concerns or questions. Please list them here. Then check back here after reading the book. Check off anything answered. It would be best if you actually wrote in the answer, so it is not forgotten in the heat of a congregant asking the same question. Then, contact me at info@orgstrat.net if you have further questions.

1._____

2._____

3._____

4._____

5._____

6._____

7._____

2 ANSWERS TO IMPORTANT QUESTIONS

Many people have questions that must be answered immediately, before they are willing to contemplate a mission to young children. Questions include: liability, inconvenience, expense, space, expertise, and congregational sentiment. These are all important, so let's address them right away.

Liability

Some churches worry about the liability. Won't the liability be large if a child gets hurt? Won't someone decide to sue at some point? Others worry about the inconvenience to older members. For instance, will the kitchen will be in use when they want to have a funeral dinner? Whether the building is suitable is a real concern. Most of these concerns can be met. As usual, the best thing is to look at the importance of mission and being willing to serve the Lord and His lambs, despite inconvenience and risk, and then *look for solutions.*

Liability can be avoided reasonably well, or corporations and individuals would not run daycares. The way to avoid liability is to 1) run the center according to standards 2) make it a separate corporation from the church, 3) buy liability insurance and 4) invest in expert help. There is never any risk-less activity, but risk is manageable if taken seriously. Too many churches run sloppy centers and ignore state rules and then are hurt and surprised when they are cited. This is unnecessary but adds to the rumor mill. Indeed, there are people who simply seek to attack others through lawsuit, but judges typically are not fooled. Any parent using the childcare will be signing agreement to the policy statement. All employees, similarly, must follow the policies and will be trained in following regulations of the state and policies of the center. The church preschool will have legal documents insuring this. Every center should have an attorney and invest in expert consulting. Learn to do things well. Further, besides the protection of in fact keeping children as safe as humanly possible, and the protection of insurance, the protection of legally sound policies and repetitive training in them, and the protection of honest jurors, we should trust the Lord, also. Isn't that right?

Adequate Facilities

Space considerations are real. Most churches have adequate space by re-using Sunday School and Fellowship Hall space, while perhaps only improving their outdoor play space. Children need space and the state requires a certain minimum square footage both inside and outside. It is complicated enough that I do not want to quote the figures here, but they are clearly written out in the Minimum Standards of each state. Every state publishes its requirements. I will give you a basic minimum rules of thumb in this small book. Later you can be sure that your facility meets the detailed requirements of your state.

Please notice, these are considered a *minimum*. Because children stay in this space full time, rather than for one hour, more space *may* be needed than for some Sunday School programs. Further, larger classroom size permits more effective placement of staff. I want to have two adults seeing one another at all times, so I prefer larger classrooms. This is better for safety and cuts costs in the long run. At the same time, the very best centers rely on larger classrooms because of their multi-sensory philosophy. So the larger classroom, with more people and more equipment is all around preferable to the smaller classroom, smaller class size, one teacher and fewer toys, relying on a paper focused, teacher-led curriculum. By the way, classrooms can be rearranged. Your Sunday program may enjoy larger classrooms and even more broadly grouped children. No doubt they will certainly appreciate better furnished rooms!

Even a church that has insufficient space might easily enough add a temporary building or two and end up with stellar, large classrooms that will later accommodate Sunday School growth or simply avoid the problems of shared space.

There are other requirements such as number of bathrooms and sinks. Further, there are practical considerations that are hard to specify such as safety of the children walking from one place to another. Normally, the licensing representative should help in planning, and in most locations there are retired representatives who are happy to act as consultants in preparing for visits from the authorities.

Shared Space

Shared space can be inconvenient. Most inconveniences can be handled through practical solutions. The very few remaining should just be tolerated because of the enormous benefit that accompanies the inconvenience. We will discuss handling shared space more in depth later in this book. Two dynamics take of these problems. First, a vision of the preschool as a mission of the church rather than as a inconvenient tenant. More children, more families, and more traffic really are good problems to have. Not wishing to have them comes from a focus diverted from the gospel – or some secondary pinch that has not been managed well. The second dynamic consists of practical management techniques. The obvious first one is strict adherence to separate shelving. When this cannot be obtained, two separate sets of locks and keys suffice. There are shelves that fold and latch for teaching toys, so that the preschool's toys will not be visible to the children in religious education. I can imagine in the few churches where a shelf of this nature for each classroom is out of the budget, but in such a case, there might be some inexpensive human help to properly re-arrange teaching toys before Monday morning is also needed. We will consider this topic of shared space more at length later, but more people in the church's programs really is not a problem.

Expense

"What about the great expense?" some object. "What about the great financial gain?" is the answer. It is true that there must be an initial outlay. The more substantial that initial outlay is, the better the center will look on its opening day and so the faster it will rocket to full enrollment and the higher tuition it may charge. Like any business, it does take an initial outlay to begin, but businesses do not consider that outlay to be an expense, but rather an investment, an asset. Assets are things that last, that make money.

Your congregation may or may not have the idea that the preschool will earn a profit. Perhaps your tuitions will be intentionally low, or you may offer so many scholarships that you will only break even. In such a case, you might consider the initial outlay to be missionary spending. Missionary spending may be outflow, but is also not considered an expense but rather an investment in the Kingdom.

Profits are attainable. Many churches charge their non-profit center rent, thus defraying utilities and building wear and tear. Some consider their center an employment boon. Some simply make a profit. I know a church, a small Episcopalian church not far from the central city, that for many years devoted itself to supporting a great full-time preschool. Now for some years, the center has been supporting the church. The preschool is robust, and well thought of – a lasting legacy. Indeed, I doubt the church would even exist today without the preschool. If others provide childcare for profit, there is certainly no reason why a church can not sustain at least break-even finances. Of course, there is some initial outlay, but most churches get regular returns, even if the original aim was missionary.

Membership Recruitment Or Conflict?

Unfortunately, only a very few churches obtain membership recruitment from their CDC, but that is because very few have good communication between the church and school. The church can and should invite school parents to church activities. Church personnel may introduce themselves at school functions. The typical split between school and church is simply a product of the lack of good management, too little of the right kind of communication, and/or a slackening of evangelistic zeal.

Sometimes there is also a cultural gap, which is real, but which can be overcome. It is worth overcoming. Often this gap comes from a change in the neighborhood which will eventually directly affect the congregation itself. The congregation must, therefore, close the gap – or move or die. Many churches have resisted the cultural or ethnic change and had to close. A few have transitioned, often because of denominational leadership. One church I know of, with a robust preschool mission, dwindled to the point they had to sell their building, but the preschool remained, and was taken over with gratitude and competence by a new congregation. With true zeal in following Jesus, adherence to the stated mission of the congregation, the problem can be overcome. Providing a service gets people talking across that gap. In a child development center(CDC) a church can get to know the entire family on an ongoing basis, provide a relationship and hence an invitation to church and to faith in Jesus. So, while issues exist, the preschool can be the tool of re-invigorating the congregation – even in a changing neighborhood.

OH! I realize this is the first time I have mentioned the name Jesus. Well, I do hope that our Jewish friends will also consider making more preschools. I do wish to include you, friends, in our discussion. Although I may not have the correct language to speak as you would speak among yourselves, I trust your interest in education inspires you similarly to see preschools as a mission in your own way. Some excellent synagogue related centers have contributed much to our city. Indeed, in our attempts in Austin to create support for Christian directors, we invited directors from the Jewish centers also. We ended up having our meetings hosted by a CDC at the Jewish Community Center. We changed the name to the "Judeo-Christian Directors Group." Our relations were warm; our aims were aligned. There are few theological disagreements at the preschool level! In this book, I have decided to leave the name of Jesus in the text because it is so important for us. I hope you understand how deeply I might feel about the name Jesus, as I know you feel deeply too, about The Name/HaShem. I do not mean to step on toes, but am doing my best to speak as authentically as I can, from my standpoint. It is a daunting challenge to speak inspirationally to all Christians, from Pentecostals to Episcopalians, yet I would like to *also* invite my Jewish friends to this mission!

And What About Spanking?

As you suspect, you may not spank children in your facility. No matter how much one may believe in it, the government forbids it. Further, simply because you are Christian, and particularly if you are more conservative, you will be suspected of spanking. Further, I would advise you to never have anyone spank even their own children at your center, nor ever threaten spanking, or even ever speak harshly to a child. People have been fired in Texas for speaking harshly to a child. What is the definition of harshly?

Raising a voice? Even on a playground? Because you are a Christian center, you must err on the side of caution. Yes. This is a reality. Your objection that this is hard to do is well taken. That is why I want to help and why I suggest one of the first moves is to hire a very competent director. The good news is that everyone must face the same rules, so it is doable. It has to be doable. If it is not, we then will not have care and education for a large portion of our society.

Are you afraid to have a center because you might be falsely accused of spanking? Isn't this letting shadows control you? There is no sense in co-operating with *possible* persecution, beating others to it. No, stand up, communicate, and have a center.

Someone else might object that they do not want to have a center precisely because they do believe in spanking. To that one I would say, please look, *but what about all the other children, not raised in your homes*? You say, "But in the center we can't do it right." Okay, but look, every other center has the same rules. Do you not think you could do a better job than others? Okay then. Have a center.

Many of my readers do not believe in spanking. Then you do not foresee a problem at this point. Build a center, and cultivate good character! Think thoroughly about how to do this. Otherwise, you may not building a better center than average. No guidance in life and no boundaries will mean no character development, more wasted, unhappy lives, and a worse society. One of the most important things congregations offer is character development.

Neither is the bathroom controversy a reason to fail to have a center. It is not likely that this tide, however strongly pushed, will come to you within the next 10 years. Indeed, the very fear that it will come at all is itself a reason to have a center. The alternative is to let children go without care.

If all centers are like what you fear, then in what society will your grandchildren live? *The only answer is to promote a movement of*

(Judeo-)Christian child development centers. Do you see? All objections are based on fears that paralyze, the only answer to which is to make centers – great centers -- and encourage your colleagues to make such centers as well.

Problems Of Hiring

The real need is experienced personnel with vision. Most churches do not have sufficient expertise to run a childcare center or school with state regulators "breathing down their necks" without some hiring from without. Yet the problem of hiring from outside runs the risk of losing vision. This obstacle can be overcome. Please understand this dilemma as a serious problem, and then work to solve the problem. Let me illustrate.

I know a well funded non-profit who took as its aim the opening of Christian CDCs in disadvantaged neighborhoods, competing directly with Head Start. They hoped to send children off to public school with a cohort of other saved, academically competent children, thus beating Head Start's results. Their prospectus put evangelism clearly at the core of their mission: getting children saved in this environment would be like "shooting fish in a barrel," it said. Obviously, they were aiming at creating an evangelical mission. Then they hired a director from a neighboring liberal mainline church. Doubtless she had run an educationally enriched center, but she told me, when I asked about evangelism because I had heard nothing of the sort from her, "Oh, if I just get the mothers reading to the children, I think I will have done great. That's sufficient." About the prospectus, she said, "Oh *I* did not write that." Divergence in vision! The center will be run to regulations, but not in line with the vision of the founding organization.

On the other hand, I know a church that had to shut down their center. I walked into those rooms, still being used for church events. I saw very few books and very few toys. I saw that no places to pin up artwork. Even the rare purchased preschool art item was placed in a way that suggested no one had thought of children. Normally you might see a chart of the days of the week, posted on the wall, but low enough for children to see and next to a rug for circle time. Here, it was posted at an angle, at adult eye level. Apparently, they had failed to hire anyone who had a background in early childhood. No wonder they didn't have sufficient students! Parents were not "buying it." The center could not begin to compete with more professionally run centers in town. The church staff may have had an evangelistic vision, but they did not have people with enough education or talent in child development to make it real.

Worse, sometimes these two lacks are combined, having neither vision nor competence. Consider how one church ran their own educational programs. A large church with periodic events and weekly childcare for their own staff and volunteers. For an ongoing weekly event, there was no curriculum and the hired staff had no thought of creating activities. When a new staff member told a Bible story, they asked, wide-eyed how she knew that story. It was Esther. She said that she had read it in the Bible. They just shook their heads, with big eyes. No, they didn't go to that church, but they had worked there for some time. They were just amazed at this newcomer's activity. Similarly, for a women's event of several hours, fifty children were placed in one classroom, with one toy per 4 or 5 children! And only one adult! Down the hall, popular movies provided the childcare for elementary school aged children. Imagine 200 children from age 5 through 12 in a dark room watching commercially made movies. One of these movies even questioned the faith experience! That was their Saturday church experience? The director in charge had no childcare experience. So now we have professionals in the sense that they were working in the childcare industry or public school for a living, but not in any way dedicated to excellence in child development on the one hand, and there was no injection of vision from the spiritual leadership on the other. These dynamics are asking for trouble. Please do better than this!

Another church lost its CDC. They strive to encourage its members to start businesses. Today the leadership won't say anything about their foray into having a daycare. It was closed down by the state. Undoubtedly, they had great aims for their congregation to raise their standard of living and contribute to society. They attempted to do the right thing, but just didn't have quite enough expertise to ensure a success. Neither did they hire it or learn it. It is a shame that they remain ashamed and unwilling to move forward again. Please know that both *faith and expertise* are needed.

Personnel is a major ingredient. We will take this up later in this book, but let me say now there are ways to build teams in order to get all the vision and expertise you need -- it just takes expert hiring, training, and ongoing oversight. Here are a few possibilities. Your denomination or fellowship may provide some of your faculty. You might partner with another center to either find mentoring or to plant a "daughter center" in the much the same way as we plant a new congregation. You may find mentoring for your staff in a staff down the road. You may be able to hire an experienced director away from another church and she can mentor staff and replacement directors. I teach this to directors, to pastors, and I can consult on and indeed help with hiring and team formation: www.orgstrat.net or 512-534-5425.

I can also help with ongoing staff training. Typically directors rely on the free staff training provided by government agencies – with predictable results. Better centers avoid these offerings but attend conferences by the very professional associations that are openly hostile to faith. The best centers do hire outside trainers to train their staff. Training is not only mandated by the regulations but also always a necessary ingredient to implementing and maintain your vision. It is crucial to have recorded, Christian, compliant staff orientations. It is vital to have periodic Christian, quality staff trainings. I have long offered this. (Pre-Service Training Binder 8 hour in reusable audio, exercises and tests, precisely fulfilling the Texas state regulation for the first 8 hours of pre-service training . Only $200. P. O. Box 971 Cedar Park Texas 78630.) We are also trying to form a Christian directors association that will provide not only social support to Christian directors but also conferences that will offer better training (send email to subscribe to announcements: info@orgstrat.net or look for email sign up on www.orgstrat.net). We are exploring online possibilities.

Obstacles Can Be Overcome

The obstacles *can be overcome* just as in any mission. First, however, you must see the potholes to avoid them; you must see the knots to untie them. Like in mathematics, once you understand the problems, you can solve them. Some churches may have the prayer power and the education expertise to make things go very smoothly. None, however, have everything, but it is all available, through education, hired help, and mentoring. I do not tell horror stories to suggest they are the norm, but simply to insure you do not make the same errors. Remember, that many people, many organizations, many congregations just like yours are successful every day at this same vital mission. And children are waiting.

3 COUNT THE COST AND ALSO COUNT THE RETURN

Nearly all church people decry the degradation of society, but they neglect the formation of culture. Going to church itself changes little beyond the church. Very little, indeed, is changed even for church members if discipleship is not a focus. Changing the people who come to church might have some effect on the those they know. Voting might change a few things. Pulling some adults from the wrong track to the right surely is a great thing. Changing the life of a child, however, changes a whole stream of people and events downstream. Training a group of children together better ensures that good character remains in each, because of the social support, peer pressure. Changing groups children and helping their parents, over time, can change the neighborhood. Developing national leaders can create a turn-around in a society.

It is upsetting to have seen a couple of decades of dramatic devolution in the skills and maturity of entering college freshmen. I do hope that senior university professors see a different picture, but I have no confirmation of that. I suppose that we have always looked to our private school elite for future leadership and I was teaching in a community college. Surprisingly perhaps, in my classrooms, it was home-school graduates who shined. Only they had initiative and diligence, the readiness to study and the manners to lead. As difficult as it may be to swallow, public school graduates are not being formed with initiative and diligence today; in fact, the reverse is systematically cultivated. An upside-down set of values is instilled in them. Even if some are bright and able and a few remain academically uncrippled, still, it is a sure bet that we will not be able to count on the mass of public school graduates to lead us out of our current troubles, but rather only further in. The majority of public school graduates are not prepared even for junior college level work! We may have some private school graduates who are capable of learning and leading, but at best they will be relatively few. Our country needs help now, and the future looks even more bleak from the perspective of character and skill. We are on the cusp of overwhelming technological power, collapsing monetary system, and looming war. Yet we have lost the very dynamics that brought us the best and restrained the worst. The worst dynamic of all is that the students have no sense that anything is wrong and they are not able to receive correction. Something must change *dramatically.*

You can make that change. You can dramatically improve grades, lives, even personalities. You can rescue kids off the street and all the bad things that could happen to them there and away from online porn or possible sexual depredation all by an after-school program. You can create a cadre of future leaders in a church school. You can even form personalities with a preschool program. You will change destinies. You can make a big difference in the life of a young single mother. If conversion is important, how much more discipleship? Education is the only way to change a culture.

The gain is enormous, more than can be counted, and yet it is attainable. So, if the reward is awesome, what is the required investment? Can we calculate that? Yes.

The first practical thing to realize is that in every state, **a license is required** to have a childcare center. In Texas, caring for more than 5 children not your own even for one half a day is a felony. So the even the women who run childcare only for the yearly football game have to have a license. So the grandmother who takes in 3 of hers and 3 others has to be at least registered (licensing "lite.") If you keep children for 4 hours or more, give them a variety of activities, and take money, you have to have a license.

There is an exception. If you run a single-focus group, like a Sunday School/Children's Ministry program, karate school, you do not need a license. **So, if you run a religious education only school, you do not need a license. This is how Sunday Schools and catechism classes do not need government approval in the United States.** There are some black churches that run leadership academies on Saturdays for their members under this rule. Power to them.

On the other hand, state regulators have been frightening when they have come investigating unclear situations. For instance, a strict sect, on an isolated farm, ran a school for its resident members' children only, with no money changing hands. After many years of running the school openly, the authorities threatened them with prison for violating the licensing requirement. Eventually, they were ruled a co-op, thus escaping prosecution. In another case, some homeschooling parents are cooperating to provide a school like environment in a church building. They armed themselves with layers of legal counsel. Everyone watching expected them to be shut down and repeatedly told them so. So far, they are still running.

If these are cautionary tales, they are also encouragements. Be sure you are within the law. Hire legal counsel that can communicate that. Be sure any advertisement is clearly complaint, too. Be active politically. Why is the government, in this country of all countries in the world, cracking down on good academics and rare moral education? Why, in a time of calls for evidence based educational philosophy, are church schools and homeschooling questioned? If standards are objective and fair, then meeting them should provide safety.

In Texas, licensing requirements for more than 12 children, outside of a home, that is, a childcare *center,* are significant. The requirements for after-school centers are often not so great as for preschools. Schools and private schools have regulations too, but less tight than daycare centers. Public school even less. I expect most states to have similar, if not stricter standards than Texas. However, the good news is that it is doable if others do it.

It is true that regulations are significant. Gone are the days when the health department turning a blind eye was all that was needed. The standards have gotten increasingly strict. Some owners have even closed up shop, and all complain. I was in a meeting where some of the best directors in the metro area yelled at a licensing representative because the regulations at that point had become both onerous, ambiguous, attached to such possibly ominous penalties. There has been some improvement since then. It is true that Licensing representatives will make surprise visits to insure compliance, but typically, only an infrequent schedule. It is true that they are harder on wealthier, whiter, and more religious centers. It is true that sometimes they do not have the same standards across the state -- even if they adamantly deny this. It is true that a teacher can be charged with something and never teach again. Some owners have been put in the position of firing their best employee or closing down their center. However, given that there are some centers that are grossly bad, inspections are warranted. Furthermore, in most cases requirements are met, and any citations are simply dealt with by complying. The fact is that all centers are under the same requirements and most meet them. Indeed, without some standards, many centers would slip to sub-par. I remember such centers when I was beginning my work life. So standards, themselves, must be welcomed.

It is possible that persecution will happen. No question, there are some people who assume that Christians are *the* social problem in our society. It is true that sometimes licensing reps make up rules to cite against. This happens. I have heard reports that some become petty tyrants. This happens. However, a multitude of centers manage. The risk is worth taking. For those who fear pervasive and increasing persecution, let me ask, what is the alternative to your acting? Inaction through fear? Isn't that like cowering in the corner when there is a necessary fight? A few of my readers may be worried about an anti-Christ beast government rising. I would suggest that in such a case the question becomes whether we wish to unilaterally cede the territory to the anti-Christ even before he appears? Really, if we are afraid that some anti-Christ force will oppose us, then surely that in itself is reason to stand up. The risk in starting a center is worth taking. I remember R. W. Schambach saying: "When they start indicting Christians, may there be enough evidence to convict me!" If you are worried about tyrannical representatives, then, imagine, how great it would be great if there were more folks who felt called to be licensing reps! Whether you consider this "part of taking the Education Mountain" or a reformation idea of vocation for all, it is a more reasonable option than simply doing nothing because of fear.

Whether the difficulties are merely random or a gathering pattern does not matter. Running a center can be done. Indeed, it is done by normal people regularly. There are some people who just start a corporation, throw up a center, wait till something bad happens, close down the center officially, then on paper make a new corporation and are open the next week-- repeatedly. If bad centers persist, then it is certainly possible for a better center to exist. *It is possible to run CDC even in face of considerable regulations.*

What might be the resistance from the congregation itself? Fear and apathy? Desire for alternative goods? Perhaps you can lead them in mission and discipleship by repeating an aspirational vision. Perhaps you can open their eyes to the benefits of education as a mission. As much as I prefer Biblical exhortations, sometimes we have to play the song list of WIIFM (what's in it for me). A daycare can improve the reputation of the congregation in the neighborhood. A daycare can improve the kinds of kids who will be in the neighborhood 10 or 15 years from now. An educational mission will improve the society and leave a good legacy – better than a well-decorated church parlor ever will.

And it can make money.

I did hear of a wonderful story from the People's Republic of China, where the church currently is in a bewildering situation of spotty persecution mixed with benign permission. In one city the government demanded the churches shut down, threatening to send in the police. They were stunned when the response was that there were 250,000 to 300,000 children in that city taking religious and moral training every Sunday, and so if the churches were to be shut down, the children would be brought to the police station every Sunday for their training. The authorities agreed that it was better that the children should be trained in morality and citizenship at the churches rather than being brought to the police station. So the churches stayed open.

Perhaps we, too, can see a tipping point where better education institutions will no longer be persecuted by governmental authorities. Again, working toward this aim is better than cowering in a corner. Anyone who is tasked with being an ambassador for the King of the Universe should be not cowering, but towering. How might we take steps toward such towering service that we would be the major influence in our society?

4 DISCOVER AND PLAN

First, consider your space because this will be the primary factor in which plan you choose. Do you have an adequate facility for classroom and play space? Is your building and yard safe, or can you make it so? (If not, imagine the pay off, even, of improvement for your existing programs!)

The first consideration is adequate square footage per child to satisfy the state's minimum standards. Measure the rooms in your building. For Texas in 2015, 30 square feet per child and 80 square feet outside is required for a licensed childcare center or an after-school center. (Notice that these and other specific requirements may change.) Do you have the square footage?

For instance, let's do a paper napkin level plan for 100 children aged two through five. For playground space, you may want two playgrounds, maybe one 1,000 square feet, and another 7,500 square feet. You may already have it. Think play equipment that is safe and provides a good view of the children, with soft surfaces anywhere they may fall. This is a significant cost but may last a lifetime. Think a four-foot fence with a gate that adults can easily open, but that children cannot.

Now let's plan for inside space. Think that for 100 children you will need 3,000 square feet in total, assuming that all your children are in attendance full time. (Half-time preschools often offer TTh or MWF hours, so they may need less space.) Notice however that your space requirements interact with your teacher/student ratio and so impact your budget. Your teaching method impacts space considerations too. For instance, using the Montessori Method will need more space than using a paper curriculum like Abeka. For both of these reasons (better staffing and more active and well stocked classrooms) , as well as for simply more calm, I prefer larger rooms. For this reason, we are doing only a preliminary investigation at this point, and will revisit space needs later.

So, if you have three classrooms each 20 feet by 25 feet, each may hold 15 children. Fifteen four year olds may be a fine number for an experienced teacher. However, you will have maybe only 12 two- year-olds together, and maybe only 8 toddlers in a classroom. But then you realize that both to reduce liability and to improve education and safety, to say nothing of teacher training, you want to have two teachers together always. Some centers seem to manage with smaller rooms, but if you have larger rooms, you may accommodate more children still staffed with just two teachers.

In a classroom 40 foot square, you might accommodate 30 children, aged 3 to 6, with the same two teachers. A 40 foot by 40 foot classroom can legally accommodate 53 children in Texas. While one or two staff with 50 children actually worked many years ago, given the change in children, very few would suggest doing that today. But if you put even 30 children, staffed with two (or three or even four adults), then you have improved the situation tremendously, insuring that a teacher will never be alone. Most probably you have also insured better teaching and budgeting by providing for more creative grouping. You have also reduced your ongoing costs. You capital outlay may not be any larger. You are accommodating the same number of children in the same number of square feet. For Sunday School purposes, if you wish smaller classrooms, you may but a folding divider wall in to bisect the room.

The centers built by individuals have often opted for smaller classrooms and ended up with staffing straight jackets. For instance, to lower initial outlay, one owner converted a house. But classrooms were so tiny that the rooms were over filled with children, who worked too much at tables, and she could not afford to place two teachers in each class.

By contrast, the best schools tend to provide larger buildings and end up with more flexibility in terms of staffing and ratio, as well as generally more space per student, *which allows for more equipment and more calmness and thus fewer behavior problems.* If you take a visit to a well-run Montessori school, you should see large classrooms, two adults, several work areas for children, and quiet, engaged children. The noise level in such a school is amazingly low . Children feel less upset and settle in to focusing on their work. Thus, they learn more, and everyone is happier. Larger rooms are very valuable.

Indoor play space is very welcome too, and especially needed in locations where the weather is often severe. If you have a fellowship hall of 50 by 50 (that is, 2,500 square feet) that is enough for 83 children at a time, under current regulations here in Texas. For active play, more would obviously be better. Probably in reality, only one class would come at a time and so make your existing space workable.

You need the same sort of staffing for playgrounds as you do for classroom activities, and maybe more. Of course, playgrounds are places where accidents may occur, so adequate supervision is vital. Since, bathrooms built for access from the playground are rare, you will probably need a third staff person available to take a child inside to the bathroom.

To imagine what that looks like, imagine a building where a fellowship hall is bounded by rows of classrooms. The classrooms double as preschool rooms, and the fellowship hall is used for assemblies, gymnasium, staff meetings, parents' gatherings, etc. Ideally a couple of doors lead directly to the playground(s) at the back of the building, without having the children walk where they can escape or encounter a moving care. Ideally, the playground also has doors directly to a bathroom, so that staff can watch both the child in the bathroom and the children on the playground.

A potty for every 16 children, is currently required in Texas. So if you had 100 children, you need about 7 potties. These must be accessible from classrooms *and* from the playground. To the extent they are not easily accessible, then you need more staff, so location is very important. You would like a staff member never to be by him- or herself while pottying children. This may be accomplished if the staff member stands outside of the bathroom where another teacher can see her. This works perfectly well when the potty is adjacent to the playground, so that both teachers see one another and both can see the children on the playground. But imagine the scenario when you have a full class on the playground and only two teachers, and then one or more of the students must go to another area to potty. Now you have a staff ratio problem -- and a possible safety problem. It is possible to call floater or office staff to escort children to the potty, but then that staff member may be by herself in the bathroom with the child. So plan not only for adequate number of potties, but also consider their locations.

Adequate plumbing is necessary where there will be diaper changing and useful wherever there is art and snacks. Where bathrooms are a little too far away, there are cabinets made to be change tables in classrooms, that can dispense water and hold water for dumping. A similar cabinet could also double for handwashing and art, but still you can see that plumbing to each class is preferable.

Note, too, that you occasionally have an independent young student who will attempt to go exploring... meaning: escape. What kind of fence to you have? What obstacles are between the classroom and the playground? Most purpose-built facilities have a door from the classroom to the playground, so that the playground hugs the building on as many as 3 sides. Consequently there are no avenues of escape – or inappropriate entry. This plan also provides two fire escape doors: one to the hall and one to the playground. So planning the space carefully helps both in terms of ongoing budget and protecting the center from later citations by the regulatory folks. It is possible that staff can escort children from one building to another, or across a parking lot, but it is much better if the building has immediate access to the playground. Appropriate fencing can often take care of the problem. Plan on using fences 4 feet high with adult only openers. Again, your weekend program will benefit too.

Another safety issue is controlled entry. Having only one entry point that is monitored, often by the director having her office beside it, is necessary. Today, many parents like an even more technologically controlled entrance, with key codes or security guards. While few churches were planned with this in mind, increasingly some parents like similar security features on their children's ministry facility as well. Check-in Counters can do double duty. If your church is large enough to have hired security, an electronically monitored entrance might be possible.

The space needs to be safe. These are the basics. Without this, you can't do anything. So evaluating the space is the first step. I can help, and so can regulators or retired regulators who become consultants. Remember that temporary buildings with potties and sinks installed can be ready made classrooms where city permits.

If it looks like you can overcome the space hurdle, then go to the next step. Alternatively, look for space elsewhere. Often there are daycare buildings and older church buildings for sale. Many once grand church buildings are becoming empty in the center city, precisely where missions are most needed. Perhaps a CDC could be part of a inner city mission or a multi-site initiative. Do not presume that all is well in the used building, but inspect thoroughly with a consultant, based on current regulations.

Further, it is my opinion that opening a CDC in a new neighborhood, and using its gym on Sunday for worship is a great way to plant a new church or new multi-site location. Indeed, I have recently discovered that I am not the only one who ever dreamed of buying a building that was built as a CDC, and using its gymnasium as a sanctuary until a larger one could be built, all the while using the daycare building as Sunday School space! It is being done!

If your building does not suffice, then consider another educational venture, such as an afterschool center. In this case, the most important issue is the proximity to the elementary school – or the ability to transport children. I have seen centers open in a slum area where children walked or were driven considerable distance, but having the congregation's building next to the elementary school is ideal for this plan.

A building that won't support any kind of children's program can still be a library and meeting place for home schooling families. They often need library and meeting space such that surely any congregation might provide.

Further, in an extreme example of not being able to house a center, a string of in-home centers may be created, with a church hosting professional association, thus providing care for many and a business for some, but still extending the mission.

Demographic/Market Assessment

I assume that you have some idea of the needs of your neighborhood, but a thorough inquiry is always helpful. How many children? In what family economic circumstances? Often segments are overlooked. Much of this information will be online. Your city may have more information. Your door-to-door efforts will always pay off. Do not be shy about meeting other CDC owners and other charity missions. Find out what is needed and what is available in your area.

Facing The Regulations

After this preliminary consideration of space, find and thoroughly read the regulations. There you can double check your assessments. Every state has its own regulations. They should all be accessible. In Texas there are sets of rules: one for in-home care, another for centers not in homes, and more for those who keep children overnight. Often the rules for an after-school center are separate and less rigorous than are those child development centers. Schools may have fewer regulations, but usually have to comply with CDC licensing requirements in that portion of their school that houses children less than 5 years old.

You should be able to find the regulations posted online. Some states offer periodic training or inquiry meetings. Sometimes these orientation presentations are now condensed and posted online. In Texas you can go to local introductory lecture days put on by the Department of Family and Regulator Services, or you might find them online at http://www.dfps.state.tx.us/. While you are there, you can search for centers in your town, find out what citations they have been demerited with and other information about them. Use this to find ideas and mentors. I believe that you will feel relieved after you make this study. You will discover than running a center is possible. Indeed, you may find that you can excel.

I recommend that you also talk to neighbors and colleagues with centers. As with any similar venture, the laments often come from those who know less, so you want to find those who know more and can be greater advisers. Take laments as cautionary tales, but take advice only from the most successful.

This book can only be an introduction; Do read the regulations. Get the online course. Be part of a support group. Indeed, you are best advised to hire someone to advise you. You will want to also hire someone excellent to help you with implementation. Then You will want someone who has an expert eye for complying with every detail, and excelling in helping children and families, as you go forward. Consulting is available, training on how to work with a consultant is available, and tips on hiring a director follows later.

Next, get the application form from your state, fill it out, be sure to comply with everything. Don't send it in until you have completed all your planning. You should be sure about your plan before asking for governmental approval. Hiring an experienced director when you start is a must. You might want to hire a director now so she can shepherd the process. Then after applying, plan to wait as much as nine months before receiving a license and opening, depending upon the state.

In Texas, a center may not advertise, let alone start, until after receiving a license. This may be the biggest challenge start ups face: keeping space rented and empty with an employee idle while waiting for the license. A church may avoid the former problem is their building is already in use weekly. You may be able to hire your director for the startup work while she is still employed elsewhere, with an agreement for a future switch. If you work well with an experienced Licensing representative, you may be able to time your opening at the beginning of a school or calendar year. Normally the representatives are not unsympathetic. Just know this delay is a possibility going in, and be prepared. Once again, understanding the problem better allows you to solve the problem.

Business Plan

Draw up a tentative business plan, including market analysis and budget. We can help you with this process if you desire (info@orgstrat.net 512-249-7629). So can business consultants.

As you write the business plan, you must figure out how many children your space accommodates, what staffing you will need, what hours and months you will be open. You will of course have to comply with any employee regulations. All this goes into expense calculation. Then also find out what the range of tuition is in your area. Do your first calculation with every child paying average tuition. Then you will begin to see where you must or might adjust. Can you afford some scholarships? Will tithing members pay the same as others? (These questions we will discuss later.) What level of quality and what level of charity do you desire? Will work for the neighborhood? There are many questions that you may not have resolved, but do begin with a basic budget. Remember that someone else down the street does this for a profit, so be encouraged that you can make things balance out.

Beyond a budget, you will want to make a mission statement, ad cast the vision. The first chapter should become some basis for that. The you will make a governance plan, pick a curriculum, make a floor plan, and gather helpers. Let's cover these next.

5 ORGANIZE AND IMPLEMENT

Organization

Normally creating a separate 501(c)3 nonprofit is the way to go. The process normally begins with registering a name for your business (getting a d/b/a) -- after being sure no one else is using that name. In Texas, the county clerk will have a way for you to search for others using the name and offer you a form to register yours. For some direction for your particular state, please see https://www.legalzoom.com/articles/dba-state-requirements/all Then take your certificate of assumed name, to request an Employer Identification Number (EIN) from the Internal Revenue Service, and then obtain state incorporation papers, and only then request the 501(c)3 from the IRS. For more information, please see https://www.usa.gov/start-nonprofit. How you name your school depends on marketing considerations in your community. If you fill out all the forms correctly with no "red flag" language, you should not have a great deal of difficulty the paperwork. Only the initial 501(c)3 does take time and effort. Sometimes there are other organizations such as denominations or ministerial fellowships that permit your corporation to be a chapter of their 501(c)3, making the process much easier and quicker.

Specify how the preschool will relate to the church. Getting governance right at the outset will prevent many problems later.

Some denominations have set rules, but normally, it is best if you have a separate board, and stipulate clearly how it is related to the church. For instance, you may require that a member of the church board of the Children's Pastor be a member of the preschool board, and require that there be at least one of the parent board members be also church members. You may wish to make the Pastor an ex officio board member or Standing head of the Nominating Committee. However, do not make your preschool board 100% church members at the expense of getting good governance. You need experienced board members and good fundraisers. It is possible to specify what kinds of decisions must come to the church for a ratifying vote. Further, the constitution and by-laws should be written so that the mission and intention of the original project are defined clearly. Be sure there are avenues of correction if the center veers from that vision. Be sure that there is yearly board training. Finally, be sure you have a director that will work with you – and then work with her. She should direct, but the board should oversee policy and raise funds, along the lines of the vision and policy of the church board.

I have seen perhaps every imaginable mistake being made in the interface between center and church. I have seen pastoral staff and church boards mess up centers. I have seen them run off the best directors in town. I have seen churches take so much from centers that they cripple the center. I have known of a director that embezzled a center. I have heard of a pastor needlessly publicly besmirching the center director who started and ran things at cost to herself. I have often seen directors veer wildly from church aims. I have seen churches make certain their centers were poorly run by making bad personnel decisions. I have seen churches neglect centers. I knew of a center that was in danger of being closed down by licensing because the church blocked building repairs. I have heard of elders harassing and threatening a director thinking that she was costing them money, when in fact the center was their only profit center. I have seen center directors pretend great loyalty and run poor centers. Of course, I've seen a church bigwig require that their child or grandchild get special treatment, have obstreperous kids, and neglect them. All these were overcome – eventually. So yes, there should be good governance, continual communication, and respect both ways for the expertise of the needed partners.

The one thing that the state does not inquire into very much is curricula, (except to insure a that you have a non-discriminatory center). They will want to see your advertising plans to insure you welcome everyone. They will want to see that your staff is trained in how to partner well with parents. The main requirements have to do with health and safety. They will want to see specifics about how diapers are changed and how toys are sanitized. Authorities sometimes require specifics that are not best, wisest, or most current practice: such as relying on bleach only for disinfecting, requiring all children have milk daily, requiring babies sleep on their backs and pushing universal vaccinations. An experienced director will be able to take all this in hand, ensure it is accomplished to the state's satisfaction and nevertheless satisfy parents. Perhaps your director will be able to contribute to the discussion as we flow through the controversies and ever changing expectations.

It may be impossible, however, to *never* be cited. The good news is that everyone has to cope with the same system. The regulations are substantial, and yes, licensing representative can and will sometimes make up rules on the spot and cite you based on those. The good news is, whether you failed in some detail nor not, or even missed something relatively important, this will not necessarily mean the end of your center. Citations, both significant and insignificant, are posted online, however. The aim is to allow parents to see how their center ranks. Normally less serious violations are satisfied by complying. More serious violations are met with remedies and penalties. There are a few cases where personnel have to be fired and only in extreme cases are centers closed down. Of course, you would want to fire an employee who abused a child, rather than wait to see if the problem happened a second time. You would want egregiously bad centers closed down. I have heard of only one story in 20 years of training and consulting where a director thought she had to unfairly fire a teacher. However, I have never seen a center closed down that should not have been. I have heard of some of these very centers just starting up again with a new legal corporation. So, the bottom line here is please aim for a squeaky clean record, do not be surprised if you are not always treated quite as well as you would like to be, but do not expect to be shut down for no reason. *In short, if you work at it, you can make it.* Young mothers may indeed check out the posted citations when considering which center to use, and this is a good thing. They *should be* comparing, and shopping for the best care. I have every expectation that you will be one of those best options.

In your planning, make a time-line, to be sure prerequisites are done when needed. Components follow.

Checklist

- Faith and vision for missional service
- Community needs assessment
- Regulations: State and maybe local health department and local fire marshal
- Space requirements, in and out of doors, as well as traffic flow
- Plumbing requirements and any other architectural requirements
- Plan for hours and staffing
- Plan for room layout and capital outlay for durable equipment
- Plan for hiring
- Marketing plan
- Budget
- Fund-raising plan
- Governance plan
- License application
- Patience

After your preliminary assessment of your building, check your community's needs. What percentage of the population has children and how many are likely under-served? What are the thoughts of the young moms about preschool education? How well are the commercial centers serving? What do your congregation's mothers say?

_____ SES breakdown and how it compares to your congregation
_____

_____ Ethnic breakdown and how it compares to your congregation _____

(Later you will address how you will meet any challenges you discover.)

_____ % of single mothers in your neighborhood

_____ % of high school mothers in your neighborhood

_____ # of daycares and how many children they hold (info is likely online at state regulatory authority's site)

_____ Philosophy of these centers (on their websites)

(If something is lacking, can you provide it? Or, if the community is satisfied with those philosophies, how will you persuade them of some other? Don't be discouraged that you are different; this may be the very best selling point that you have!)

_____ How many on state funding (CCMS in Texas) and what kinds of difficulties the directors are having with it ? (Find a friend who can inform you)

____ ____ ____ What is tuition, and what is the range?

What is the wage scale? broken down by kind of center

    In home with up to 5

In home with up to 12

Infant

Privately owned

Corporate

Elite

Then check your space against regulation requirements. Make room and playground layout plans and purchasing lists. Room size influence staffing decisions, which, along with equipment needs will determine budget and fund-raising needs.

Architectural requirements go beyond having enough square footage and enough potties in the right area. You need safety and functionality. You will want beauty, good light and greenery, and a warm, happy feel.

The fire marshal will have regulations as well as the state authority over CDCs. Of course you have fire extinguishers and probably have sprinklers but the requirements might be higher for childcare centers than for churches. You must have a rear exit with "panic bar" opener, so that people may exit quickly. Your fire marshal may require *each room* to have a second exit. Some may permit exit from a window in case of fire. I do recommend windows that can be opened in every classroom if at all possible. There is research that shows that access to the outdoors calms children and helps them focus on academics! Besides, ventilation is always nice.

You already have a plan for traffic flow, I presume. Consider if you have a funeral or other event at the same time as children are being picked up from school. Please consider security when you think of traffic flow. Plan for parents passing by the director's office and signing their children in and out. Clip boards on the top of dutch door ledges are one way to accomplish this. There are new electronic ways, but I can hardly imagine them being as reliable in a crisis as the old clip board. Of course you must ensure against losing a child and prevent any unauthorized person picking up a child. Ideally your solution will be both safe as well as warm and friendly.

Entry must be controlled. Many churches were built in the era when we did not worry about terrorists and so have a variety of doors, access points, and so forth. For your children's center, please plan to avoid the worst. Limiting access to one front door that is always watched is standard. It will be ideal to have a reception counter or a director's office at the door to the center. This may double as a check-in facility for Sunday School. Some schools go so far as to issue electronic codes to all parents. Others provide ante rooms so that parents cannot enter classrooms, but can only see in. I prefer the type of center where parents enter freely, and are known by everyone else. The community would identify any intruder and a plan would be immediately put into action. However, the kind of access and the kind of security that is best for you may depend on your market and their expectations. Some parents will revel in the electronic pass-code and others in the community belonging.

The best centers are now built with possible terrorism in mind in other ways as well. It is better if the children are shielded from view at all times. This means that while a four-foot fence is required so children don't escape, bushes or a privacy fence might be preferable so people don't see in. Large windows are a boon in a classroom, but tinted glass or shades are very helpful. Lastly, it is ideal if you have strong structures that prevent a vehicle from driving through your wall. Planter boxes, stone benches, trees and gardens are good help in this regard. Large churches very often have their own security force these days. Your head of security, or that of a neighboring or related church, can advise you. Organizational Strategies does have a one-hour training on this, but when planning, professional advice is worthwhile: better to avoid trouble than to grieve.

Make a plan for what hours and what staffing you need. Only then can you determine your staffing budget. For instance, while a part-time preschool can start and stop at set times and so have only full staffing, making for a simple plan; most full-time daycares will have students coming in as early as 6 a.m. and leaving as late as 6 p.m. The earliest hours and the latest hours often are less well staffed since there are fewer children. Further, since it is not a good idea to plan for very long hours for caregivers, you will probably have some part-time staff for the afternoon period. You will place your most experienced teachers in the mornings. These women may wish to work only part-time anyway, if they have children still at home. Further, because of the requirements of Obama-care, most companies are trying to work with part-time only staff, and this is certainly true of church centers running on small budgets.

Make a list of desired faculty skills and traits. These will influence the level of expertise you need to hire for, and thus your budget. Your most important asset in gaining and retaining students is the quality of your staff. Do not scrimp on the quality of director(s) and lead teachers you obtain, or you will not meet your mission.

Make a marketing plan. Do not neglect this. You may be able to have a center without one, but you may have grave difficulty if you can't generate clients in a downturn. You can do this only with a marketing plan. A marketing plan provides for a regular, welcome way to demonstrate how your center is a superior value to all others. Today the gold standard for marketing is the free sample method. Since you have a great deal of material to offer on family and child rearing, if you plan a way to give some away in an attractive manner, you may make a superior sales funnel. Please contact me for consulting on this if I can help. info@orgstrat.net.

Make a projected budget. Make a list of capital investments. Make a fundraising plans or capital campaign if you need to do so. I can help you on all of these items except capital campaigns, for which I would recommend denominational/fellowship level help.

6 BUY EQUIPMENT FRUGALLY
AND SHARE SPACE HAPPILY

Of course, there is some durable equipment you will have to purchase. The good news is that the more expensive durable equipment lasts for years and that some items can be home-made or innovated. Cheaper purchases, however, often have to be replaced quickly, amazingly quickly, because the use in a CDC is heavier than in a home. Aiming for a fully stocked, high quality center is a real kindness. Affluent children are simply offered a great deal more with which to build their brains. Offering the same equipment to poor children results in untold achievement dividends.

Every center needs an outdoor play structure, and ideally two: one for toddlers and one for older preschoolers. This is your biggest single expense for equipment. If you have the budget, getting a quality items that will not have to be replaced is important; however, buying a less expensive one that will be replaced within a few years from wear and damage is acceptable as a start-up plan if you plan for that replacement. For instance, a plastic slide will have to be replaced in a couple of years, whereas the more expensive metal slide may last some decades. In any case, it is beneficial to have expert input into which one you buy so that equipment will be safe, beautiful, and pass state requirements. Typically, the state requires some soft surface underneath so that if a child falls, there will be no brain injury. Further, it is preferable to have a climbing structure that is able to be seen through, so that at no time will a child be hidden from supervision. Plan for this item to run possibly as high as $10,000. The simple metal jungle gym of the school yard, the whirligig of public parks a generation ago, and the wooden structures of backyards will not be suitable; they will not pass licensing standards. Swings are particularly problematic because they need lots of extra space and plenty of soft surface. However, if they can be accommodated, I do recommend them because they are very therapeutic to many children. Shop for new alternatives.

It is ideal to have some sort of indoor climbing structure as well, in cases of inclement weather. Some larger churches make their indoor climbing structure a focus of attention to draw the delight of their younger guests. Other churches simply make their fellowship hall available for games and gym time, without offering climbing structures. Many wonder items such as small boats that can turn over to make bridges, structures of cushions and even tree houses can be purchased for indoor classrooms.

Probably you will use your existing classroom space for classrooms. As previously mentioned, larger rooms provide more flexibility in staffing and activity centers. It is much better to have two teachers at all times rather than one. The open center idea, where one classroom teacher can see the next classroom, offers advantages in terms of safety, but a higher noise level and a higher likelihood of a child escaping has made this fashion less popular.

All classrooms need enough space so that children can move around, make choices of activities, and have some active time. Every classroom needs enough space to gather all of the children in at least two different areas. Think for instance, of the teacher reading a story to a group on the floor, while the assistant sets up a craft on the tables. If the room were so small that there was only one space, crowding would be annoying and encourage behavior problems, thus lower learning.

Every classroom will need to have space for artwork and posted educational material. Normally, every classroom will have tables and chairs at the right size for the students, and a sink, and upper cabinets for the teachers. Classrooms will need to be close to toileting facilities, and for those who may have students still in diapers, will need to have a changing table near a sink. If one cannot have these built in, it is possible to buy a changing table, a counter, and a sink (that can be filled with water and dumped) as moveable furniture.

Each classroom will need a rug for story time, a chair for the adult, and places on which to post artwork and educational material. Parents often make decisions about a center's quality based on the visual they see when they walk in. All humans, even the smallest, appreciate a beautiful environment. The décor of the center sets the stage for the quality of work.

Each classroom will need low shelves on which to offer toys, books, and educational apparatus. Toys and teaching equipment will need to be made of wood and sturdy plastic, as the home variety of toys will quickly become damaged and worn-out. Commercial grade equipment is well worth the expense.

Here are some suppliers:

www.lakeshorelearning.com

www.kaplanco.com

www.discountschoolsupply.com

http://www.childcarecatalog.com

https://www.strictlyforkidsstore.com

Montessori equipment is wonderful, even if you are not starting a Montessori classroom. The math and reading materials cannot be beaten. Neinhuis, **www.nienhuis.com**, is the original and best, but most expensive. Here are some lower priced outlets for comparison shopping.

www.adenamontessori.us

www.alisonsmontessori.com

www.montessoriequipment.com

www.montessorioutlet.com

www.montessori-n-such.com

Please advise us of any great vendors.

Invest in durable teaching equipment that you can re-use for decades rather than consumables, which in any case have questionable educational value. Ideally, each should be self-correcting, teaching one and only one idea.

Today many people think that worksheets equal academic rigor and so better education. This is not true, especially in early childhood. Having real objects teaches more than paper. Forcing the worksheet idea may indeed tire and repulse children. Further, while it may seem cheaper at the outset, in the long run, it is much more expensive. I was consultant for a church that printed various worksheets out every Sunday because they were so poor – or so they thought. When we calculated the long term cost of purchasing a full set of curricula that lasted for 3 or 4 years, that option proved to actually be cheaper than the photocopying. When parents ask for worksheets, typically they want more education and don't realize that real understanding of math or even reading might come better through manipulables. Worksheets are not the best way to obtain better education. You may wish to purchase a curriculum to ensure consistency and quality, but a good curriculum would not be mainly worksheets for preschool children.

Of course, if you have a school, the extension of school curricula may seem obvious. However, I would again caution you to consider the wider context. First, you may meet some resistance from state authorities. Most early childhood educators are used to the idea of "play based learning" but the wording in some regulations and the application of some administrators has become "play *only*" (which is worrisome dumbing down.) Therefore a paper-based, highly scholastic curricula is more likely to meet resistance than "play-based *learning*" with "didactic apparatus." Secondly, if your school is highly academic, your children may need more motor coordination training than would normally be the case. I have seen extremely well educated elementary students not be able to tie their shoes, suffer at sports, and even literally repeatedly fall out of their chairs during class. These first graders could sing more grammar and Texas history than my college freshman could identify, but doing a free-hand drawing was terrifying for a few of them. Their school is a good one, but in such a case, more three dimensional approach may be exactly what is called for in their preschool years. Small children are just not ready for paper oriented curriculum.

If your center accepts infants, you will have to have cribs and bedding of a certain quality and specification according to standard. Your staff will be thoroughly trained in your state's methods on how to prevent "crib death" or Sudden Infant Death Syndrome. In the U.S. this consists normally of requiring infants to be put to sleep on their back. However, in Australia, authorities claim that it is the flame retardant mixed with baby vomit that causes a chemical that asphyxiates the children, We know that babies can sometimes turn over, and that there is some small risk of chocking on spit up while on the back, and we in the U.S. do still have crib deaths at a higher rate than the Australians. Therefore, might ask if organic cotton sheets without flame retardants might be permitted, given you would have no flame makers close to the cribs at any time and the children are fully supervised at all times. I recommend following the law and do hope the science and conversation progresses. Having an infant to die in the center is such a tragedy in so many ways, that you will want to carefully consider every possible prevention.

Consider air purifiers and UV lights *in the AC system* for odor and germ reduction. After hours, you might use UV lights for sanitization in addition to the bleach your state probably requires. Aside from stress on plastics, this is a preferable way to kill germs, because unlike chlorine, there is no poisonous effect on children. Although many air purifiers also have mild ozoneators, I do not recommend ozoneators running while the children are present, because their little lungs are so fragile they might be harmed and the young children would not have the ability to notice and explain that there was a problem should one arise.

Natural lighting is preferable. Reggio Emelia centers stress the need for natural light, not without reason. Have generous windows and lovely garden space as well as plenty of playground time. There will probably be fewer behavioral problems because of it. Although the term "nature deficit disorder" is controversial, there is evidence that children who can see green outside their window are more calm and focused on their academics than students in a study carrel (Dunkley 2013). Your staff and your prospective customers may feel happier because of natural light. If you cannot have large windows and skylights, you might least invest in light bulbs that are natural spectrum, instead of the incandescent bulbs.

Shared Space

Many complaints and worries come from shared space. Perhaps the Children's Ministry and the preschool supplies might get mixed up. The Sunday School kids might get into the teaching materials of the preschool and so there must be continual picking up of toys and the occasional search for a missing piece. Traffic might become an issue because preschool families and church families are driving in at the same time. Worst of all, a cover for an electric plug might be taken the day before the surprise licensing inspection. These are not terrible problems but opportunities to mature in Christian character and rejoice in a flourishing congregation!

One church in Austin decided not to have a preschool because the kitchen was needed for funerals. What kind of perspective is this? Why not just coordinate? Is it too much to tell the center so they could serve sandwiches in classrooms on those days? It seems a small problem to refuse such an important mission. Everyone in a family knows you have to make allowances for other people, because without the other people, you would be bereft, without that family member. Churches with no young people decry how unfortunate it is that young people don't want to go to church.

Once when I was guest preaching, an elderly parishioner lamented to me that young people didn't want to come to church. I remembered, however, that when I was driving around trying to find the driveway of her church, I had to stop my car several times for strollers – going to the church around the corner. Inconvenience is better than lament.

So let's use any inconveniences as opportunities to polish Christian character. If the usual thesis that conservative churches are more likely to grow than others is correct, then perhaps it is because it is in those churches the leadership can more easily remonstrate for better behavior. They can take out the Bible and preach a principle in response to a petty complaint or challenge to the direction of the leadership. Whether or not this speculation is entirely correct, please let it stand as a reminder to lead people through vision rather than being cowed by complaints.

Most churches will use share space. This may not be anyone's idea of heaven, but it is entirely doable. Separate cabinets, possibly with locks are obvious. Both teachers will be trained to 1) use their own supplies and 2) be patient with the inevitability of Sunday School children handling CDC equipment. It is possible to find shelving that closes so that there is a reduction of material mess, but inevitably some Monday morning a teacher will arrive with a mess to tidy. CDC teachers will have to be told that the church is the host and provides the space. Children's Ministry teachers will have to be reminded that the CDC is an important mission of the church. Remind everyone that patience and Christian love will be called for precisely because we are together in mission.

7 HEART OF EDUCATION

CURRICULA

The decisions about curricula are more important than is often realized, even for the preschoolers. Center curricular strategies vary. Some churches with highly educated staff permit and task their teachers with coming up with their own curricula. This often works well. It gives the teachers a sense of buy-in. Many devise wonderfully creative projects. Other schools advertise a purchased or long used locally developed curriculum of which they are very proud. Many times, however, their choices are poor. Further, many new curricula are coming out. So some general advice is in order.

Firstly, simply teaching the alphabet and colors is a poverty stricken tactic. There is much more that needs to be taught! General life skills, general health and good physical skills, appropriate and creative self-expression and general information about how the world works undergirds academic learning. Further, academic learning should extend far beyond mere alphabet and colors by a huge margin! Children can learn so very many things! Indeed, they will, unless you stop them. Being unnecessarily poverty stricken, holding back brain development might not be abuse, but it certainly is not good.

Secondly, a curriculum based entirely on paper, a 2D system, is a very poor idea for preschoolers. It is not developmentally appropriate. It will inevitably frustrate a great many of the children and consequently is probably self-destructive until about age 7. Use worksheet sparingly!

Copying is only one of many methods. It is far too rigid to be the standard of preschool education. Further, preschool children will differ considerably in their development and aptitude, so copying will prove frustrating in one way or another to many of the children. I will not make a general rule that copying should never be done. What I am saying is copying should not be the main teaching method. Use it very sparingly.

Further, this 2-D approach heightens the problems in math, particularly for girls. Professor Uri Treisman, frustrated at the slow progress of female students in college level introductory physics, separated the sexes, set aside the text, and went with the women to the lab. There they rolled or slid objects down an incline before starting to talk about drag. They flew paper airplanes before they talked about lift. They threw balls and spit-wads before they talked about drag and … you get the picture. This procedure might not be necessary if there were adequate interaction at the preschool level to give each child an adequate sense of how the world, and their bodies, worked. Play, or what seems like play, is a great foundation for scientific exploration. Many kinds of hands-on investigations should be offered.

It is no surprise at this time that our children are lacking social skills. Public school was never designed to teach these, and in fact prevents social development in favor of the contingencies of mass education: stand in line, be quiet and do what you are told. Stay with a group your own chronological age. Don't question. And certainly don't be creative. All these are necessary to mass education, but none of them are helpful in preschool development, social development, or optimal whole life education. Thus, just as the block center is helpful to the study of physics, so the housekeeping center, the playground store, and the sandbox are helpful in practicing practical social interaction. Emergent projects and problem solving should furnish the child with great social skills.

Maria Montessori used a scientifically grounded, multi-sensory, individual approach that has outperformed other educational methods for more than a century. Students from Montessori schools typically have had academic performance than other students. They are often more mature and kinder than other students leaving a preschool and entering an elementary school. Most newer methods have included insights from Montessori's. However, the underlying philosophy is suspected by many conservative Christians as being too humanist. Montessori was a devout Roman Catholic and said she thought she had been inspired by God to start a system (Fidellow 2017). Besides, it is not necessary to adopt all the philosophy as it has developed to merely make good use of multi-sensory equipment. Further, Montessori has been misunderstood as an "anything goes" philosophy and this is not so. Dr. Montessori herself was appalled at American's application of her method, and told them directly that they should remonstrate, "We do not do this" rather than let children act badly (Spontaneous Activity 1965). My own observation is that Montessori schools are more quiet than other preschools because the children are more likely working with rapt attention. Secondly, the early Montessori was more informed by her Roman Catholicism, and the method has been well used by some evangelical Christians. For more on this, consult www.christianmontessorifellowship.com. Thirdly, it may be that Montessori's interest in peace and the League of Nations may have been highlighted by her more liberal proponents. In any case, I see no reason to dump so much of what the Method does well if one disagrees with these later interests. Any center could adopt at least the basic use of the sensorial, math, and language materials. If you do not, you must start from scratch finding a way to introduce to the child basic numeracy, literacy, physics, etc. You may adopt the material and the practical use of it, and even the mindset of scientific exploration without adopting the whole of Montessori's philosophy. Nothing in basic sensorial education, life skills like cleaning a table, or numeracy or literacy detracts whatsoever from a Biblical worldview. It does take a little training to present the equipment in the right way, but why an exact presentation with little distraction should be a problem, I can not imagine. Further, "freedom to do right" should not be controversial, if only understood. It is not a free for all, with "anything goes." Rather, some limited choices are presented in a prepared environment so that a child is engaged in active learning. I would urge those who are frightened about the Montessori Method to inquire a bit further by reading the original work and touring some Christian Montessori schools.

The ability to implement Montessori discipline does take time and training. Montessori did not mean that children should be allowed to do just anything, and she said that she was annoyed by this American interpretation of her work. She did say that children should have freedom – but only "freedom to do right." At that time, boys, starting at age seven were chained into desks all day while being taught Greek and Latin. She, by contrast, wanted children to quietly pick out prepared sensorial work and work on it during the morning. They may practice any learning activity that has been presented to them, or they may request a new lesson from the adult. Typically there are opening exercises first thing in the morning, and group activities as in any education institution in the afternoon.

Once Montessori's school was visited by a Roman bishop who thought that passing out cookies would engender a melee, with every child pushing to get his or her own, thus illustrating original sin. However, by contrast, the children were so fascinated by the various shapes that they were not fighting with each other at all, but exclaiming over the various shapes. At another time, she challenged the children to be as still and quiet as the sleeping baby she held in her arms. Could they do it? They all tried; it was a fun challenge to see if they could restrain themselves. The point here is that Montessori did aim for quiet and orderliness classrooms, even though she did permit movement and some choice of learning assignments. Similarly, she did eliminate corporal punishment and ridicule in her classroom but she expected a higher level of comportment and learning than her peers did. Her work balanced discipline and freedom. Today, when the standard is opposite to that of Montessori's time, it may be equally as useful as it was then, precisely because it is grounded in science and cultivates self discipline.

Even if you have a some strong preference for some other philosophy and curricula, please consider what does work in this system. The ability to deal with clothing closures, understand math, and learn to write with ease that comes easily with this material, makes it very useful. The idea of manipulables being the best teaching method for this age, verified by observable science and long practice, is universally accepted, if not always implemented. Please let me give you some pictures so you see what I mean.

Please come with me into a Montessori classroom. First, you will notice, as soon as you enter, if you are familiar with daycares, you will be astonished at how quiet the room is. The children are working. They don't know it is not play. They love learning. The two year old may choose to work on sweeping. He is then given a child-sized broom and dustpan, and some bits of brightly colored paper, so he can see what he is sweeping. He may practice sweeping as long as his interests holds. Then he must put the items back in their place and quietly choose something else to work on until called to lunch.

A two and a half year old may be working on the dressing frames, learning how to buckle, and lace and tie. A three year old may be matching colors or smells or grading weights. A four year old is tracing the shape of sandpaper letters with his fingers. One day he will reproduce that easily and without fault using a pencil on paper. Another four year old is building words with moveable letters. Another is setting out cards of simple words and matching them with pictures: "bed" with a picture of a bed. They are entering reading effortless, and early, and without tears, because each step is separate from the others.

Each step is also self-correcting, and each is presented in a multi-sensory way. A three year old is arranging cylinders from short to tall cylinders. If he puts one in that is too long or short, it is evident, so he corrects himself. Another builds a stair of long red rods, the longest measuring a meter and the shortest one tenth of that. A four year old is rearranging rods, with each decimeter in length painted blue or red, She discovers that 2 five rods when placed together have the same length as a ten rod and so forth. Later she will place cards with numerals written on them to identify the equations she is only discovering today.

A five year old is working with a 3D puzzle. Later he will discover that this puzzle is a the representation of the trinomial formula. Do you remember how hard it was to work trinomial equations in high school? For my remedial students in high school, I bring out this cube, so finally the student sees what this is. No wonder students with this sort of preschool may shoot ahead in academics later. They have knowledge of the real world in their senses, and so it makes sense in their head.

Especially when the alternative is aping a failed system, considering this time test method makes sense. Public school, in contrast to their slogans, very seldom implements scientifically based, pedagogically sound, or sensible systems. While there are a number of systems that make sense once the child can read, it is hard to imagine how to run a good program for the smallest ones who necessarily are discovering the world and human society without being a 3D system – using manipulables. Similarly, in a time when mental and physical development is even less uniform than the nature of individuality has always been, it is hard to imagine a better system allowing for working at one's own pace so that concepts are mastered while at the same time helping a child learn self-control and insuring an orderly, quiet classroom.

Another historical education whose work is helpful is John Amos Comenius, a protestant church leader form Czechoslovakia who invented picture books. Unfortunately he said little about the preschool years, and focused more on grade school. The advantage to his system was that it was very kind and it was thoroughly Christian, thus offering a good basis for Christian schools. The Comenius Institute for Leadership is K-12 school at MorningStar in Fort Mill. MorningStar, while not historically tied to Moravians, does honor that heritage. Their interpretation is one modern example of attempting to apply Comenius' philosophy.

At any rate, in all cases, there must be adequate number of toys/manipulables/didactic apparatus for every child to have at least one – at the same time! Fancy looking centers with no toys on the shelves are criminal farces. I am being too polemical? Gosh, I care about children, and I see centers that look good to parents because the architecture and décor is superior, but then I see the few toys in the center are in the display case. Educators know that "an active body makes an active mind" Scientists knew that in 1900; we are talking about that today with our seniors; educators know this. It is criminal to knowingly stunt a mind. It is a farce to have an elegant lobby and a poverty stricken classroom. Centers must have things for the children to put their hands on! May it never be that a congregation's center fails in this.

Staff Training

Staff training is of the utmost importance if you want your staff to follow your vision. Even to ensure written curricula be effectively implemented, you must ensure a great deal of staff training. There are good reasons that the government both requires training and offers it free. Notice however, that this free training is seductive. Free training may devolve into ticking off the boxes, regardless of quality. Free government training might be charitable, but it may contains elements that may be hostile to a congregation's mission. Plan for this. Be sure that your director has adequate and ongoing, quality, relevant training. Find Christian trainers. Partner with other churches to exchange ideas and keep your staff interested in progressing. Hire professionals, treat them as such, and equip them so that they can provide the quality of center you envision.

Similarly, board training is an ongoing necessity. Just as you must spend time thinking about your church board, think about your center's board. Require that there be connection and oversight with the church. It is quite possible to also get members who are helpful in terms of fundraising and reputation in the community. Good structure in the beginning will help insure mission is maintained. Get professional advice at the inception, so you can start healthy patterns. Then hire trustworthy professional training periodically so that those patterns are maintained. I do this. Your denomination may help as well. Only training can insure everyone is on the same page – and remembers that page.

8 HEART OF HEARTS - CHAPEL

Chapel is the most neglected and overlooked aspect of the church affiliated preschool. Often chapel is merely a break for the teacher and a field trip to a fancy sanctuary, with little thought of the content of presentation. It should be the center of the center. If congregationally affiliated schools are better than others, then what they do is superior. Chapel makes the difference. It is the heart of conveying the heart of what we do. Thus, we should pay particular attention to it, and it should be integrated into the every day's activities. When chapel is an afterthought, people are demonstrating that they do not believe in or care about what they are doing. They are teaching that the faith is not important! Or not connected with the rest of life!

This is not to say that everything should be rigidly religious! Sometimes the strictest group fails to connect godliness with competence. Because they eschew man's learning, they tend to eschew all learning. This is sad, destining their children to be less well-off and less influential in a culture that needs their witness. I do want fun. I do want great learning. I just say this should be intentionally connected with what is learned in chapel.

Traditional activities of chapel are wonderful educational experiences. The repetitious singing of songs and the telling of Bible stories, even if only baldly as cultural information, is helpful. Music and repetitious clapping is therapeutic for some brain dysfunctions and so probably develops brains in ways we do not yet know. We do know that telling and participating in stories is a good foundation for language arts. Bible stories are basic cultural information, moral foundations, and stand as a foundation for later theological understanding. The exhortations to self management are golden. So chapel is good. So much more awaits.

Much of our society strongly doubts the existence of good as opposed to evil. However, if one adopts this view, one has no foundation to argue for a better society. Given no boundaries of behavior, we wander into areas where we are necessarily victims and/or victimizers. Thus, a basic Judeo-Christian value set, teaching both right/wrong, forgiveness, and justice is of primary and unique importance. Given that we know that children form their personalities before seven, a more important mission than teaching children these values can hardly be imagined.

Further, just the Bible stories themselves, even as badly and disconnectedly as they are normally taught, nevertheless, could become a basis on which to understand the moral value set claims. Yet there is so much more to Bible stories than repetitions of Noah's Ark. A full chapel curriculum, integrated into the overall curricula would make for a most enriched education.

Chapel should be conducted by someone who understands the teaching of young children. Yes, of course, invite the Pastor, but do not task someone who is not "tuned into" children to regular teaching. Further, chapel should be taught with vigor, passion, and style. This is important. It is entirely possible to communicate to children the basics of your faith. They can participate – unless yours is a wholly intellectual endeavor. Even then, they can think. But notice, they can pray, worship, and interact with God! Finally, chapel should be tied to practical character lessons and applied throughout the day.

Integrating the chapel curriculum with the other academic curricula is something I have not seen. It can be done. God created the earth connects with every science lesson, every animal craft, and every art. I am not saying that you should wearily drone on about this one point; what I am saying is that these thoughts can be connected. God calls us to show forth his glory – in art, in orderly environment, in inventions, and so forth. God loves us. This should permeate everything we do in school. The children we teach are more important than even the things we teach them. God gives us good gifts. Jesus came to serve. Good triumphs over evil. If you begin to think through the faith, as ask God for guidance, you will surely see abundant connections. Let's talk about those as we go.

So, for a basic picture of how this might work, let's imagine we have read about Noah's ark. Maybe that is a great time to talk about animals. Maybe we read about Elisha's apprenticeship with Elijah and so we learn about learning, service, patience, and leadership. Maybe we have read about Dorcas' sewing. Maybe that is a great week to work on sewing projects or a charity project. Maybe when we talk about God loving us, we can introduce a song that uses everyone's name.

Indeed, the ability to integrate Bible curricula into the overall lesson planning is for me a critical aspect of hiring. I ask a candidate if she were suddenly left alone for a day and had to develop curricula, because the lead teacher had an emergency and failed to leave lesson plans, could she name a Bible story and give an example of the day's lesson plans. Often people who tell me they go to church can't name a single Bible story. Typically, I hear about Noah's Ark. If you are really hiring people who will really write lesson plans, don't accept that one! Then I ask them, given any particular story, if they can come up with a wide range of activities are at least tangentially related. If not, then do they really know anything about the Bible or have enough experience with early childhood education?

Let me try to give you some more examples. It is not hard to imagine how the Easter story might be tied to the week's curriculum. Artwork and activities would tie together, as should always be the case always. This is not to say that the entire instruction must be strictly Biblical in content, but that the Bible stories should be reinforced with other activities and that the character lessons coming from chapel should be applied and re-visited at other times of the day. For instance, Easter might be a good time to study a butterfly chrysalis. Maybe we could count to three and talk about day and night and what time means. Maybe we could count to 120, because that is how many disciples waited in the upper room. Maybe we could talk about disappointment, waiting and hope. Maybe we could talk about the walk to Emmaus. Of course, there is a lot of artwork that might be appropriate. The story of Noah's ark can go to animals, sexual reproduction, lessons about water, about swimming safety, about birds, and about how to behave in close quarters. We could even explore volume or Boyle's law by studying the measurements of the ark. I hope this clarifies: something in every area of education, from life skills, numeracy, literacy, art and science can be connected and thus reinforce the lesson. The Bible lessons should connect! Inquiry should be inviting, across the curriculum. It is all fun!

Please send me great examples of how your center have done this. Have you purchased or written a curriculum that you want to share? Have you innovated creative lesson plans attached to chapel lesson? Let's share and make this much more widely distributed. Be certain that your lesson planning, hiring, and training support the vision for the centrality of chapel in your school. Make a truly high quality, truly congregationally affiliated school.

9 BRINGING IN MONEY AND SPREADING IT AROUND

I have said it and will say it again: this mission could pay for itself. Normally we do mission without expecting the ones helped to be the ones footing the bill. In this case, it can be so. Parents pay for care and education for their children all the time. Individuals and even corporations care and educate for profit – typically as their primary motive. Our aim is greater than profit, our vision character formation of the children, service to the family, and the neighborhood, and possibly church growth, it is possible that the mission can at least pay for itself. What congregations bring that predicts better academic performance (Jeynes 2001) costs nothing, at least directly. Congregations outperform in educational mission because of caring, better educated staff, and most importantly character formation seem to be the reasons. Since many parents are looking for higher quality alternatives, it is possible, depending upon your area and strategy, that the center could earn a profit.

Of course, many of you want to make a school as a charitable mission. I do hope all the schools I encourage do have at least some scholarship slots. In any case, whether founding a school as a purely missionary endeavor or not, it is always necessary to track the monies in order to make the project sustainable. Indeed, it is a Biblical principle: "Be thou diligent to know the state of thy flocks, and look well to thy herds." Proverbs 27:3

First, work to establish yourself as a market leader. How? In the same way everyone else who is a market leader does so: have both good service and excellent marketing. Marketing is merely communication about what you are doing -- in the way, shape and form that the consumer wants to know. Apple may have superior design or engineering, but instead, they market "cool." American Express may not have any particular advantage, but we know we "shouldn't leave home without it." These are an old examples of the importance of advertising. Cult followings of information marketing is a newer example. The newest thought is 1) give away a free product or free information 2) thus becoming a welcome guest and 3) explain why your offer is a super value, 4) make a customer for life and 5) have high-end prices as well as low entry points.

Even if you do not want to make use of all of the latest marketing, please do advertise, market, and track your results. Please do give away free samples of information and tours. Please be inviting to young parents who are checking out the center. Invest in a good online presence. Young parents search online for their needs. Do not fail to invest in this communication. Also, manage your online reputation.

Be sure to welcome parents into the center warmly. Every parent should want to know the cleanliness, the friendliness, and the philosophy of your center. Some may come with contrary philosophies. Be respectful but be open about yours and be ready to provide more information. You would love to persuade them, I'm sure, so have a book or two to give them. Address a father's need for good value and a mother's need for assurance of tender care. Be sure to invite advisors to help with this communication effort. Plan ways to manage parents' reasonable desire to see the classroom and your students' need for lack of interruption. Some centers use mirrored windows and others assign a visiting adult a specific chair and tell them not to converse with the students. Many centers group their tours into bi-weekly events. No good center would entirely exclude parents from seeing it. Surely you wish to do more; you wish to make people feel welcomed.

People will want to give to your project. They certainly should. If they only knew that this would be the most important domestic mission, would impact the world that they live in 20 years in the future, and that this mission has the biggest outcome, they should run to contribute. When you are starting a program, this is a great time to tap your own members. Would they buy a book? Fund capital outlay? Contribute to the toy fund? Establish a scholarship? Be an on-call substitute?

Right here brainstorm where you can get funding. Start with folks you know. Then expand through the community. Only lastly think about granting agents. They will help, but only after other people and only after you can show some success. So that is a great idea for a capital expansion. For instance, maybe your congregation can handle fifty three- and four- year olds, but a granting agency might come up with a building after three years of your success, so that you can expand: more children, toddlers and kindergarteners. Make sure you put 20 items on your list, as this will be a good discipline to generate more ideas.

1.

2.

3.

4.

5.

6.

7.

8.

9.

10.

11.

12.

13.

14.

15.

16.

17.

18.

19.

20.

Do this repeatedly and then run your best ideas by someone else who is a better fundraiser than you. Do this together. Don't let treasurer who focuses only on frugality veto the plan; instead partner with a committee of those who are most skilled in asking for money. If you are not talented in raising funds, find someone who is. The organizational fundraiser is often most welcomed and heralded in history, because after the fact it is realized how much of an impact the "schnorrer" has had in building institutions on which we depend. Most pastors and non-profit leaders often take years to develop into brazen money gatherers out of tortuous necessity. Others seem to be born with the knack. Development professionals who are new in the profession are trained to become used to asking for gifts that are large. There is both personality and training involved. We need this talent. We can cultivate it.

There are many possible creative ways to raise funds. You are familiar with sales, galas, and campaigns. Some denominations encourage congregations to hire companies that sell bonds in order to fund a building project. At universities, they hire better students to call all the alumni yearly to ask for a donation, but the bigger money comes from the development department. There, trained professionals research the income and assets of alumni. Then, they make an appointment to call on these alumni, in their homes. Then the development officer asks for a gift. They make sure the "ask" is big enough to get a gasp from the potential donor. There may be a benefit, such as their name on a building. Plaques with donor names are common in many synagogues. Felix Adler (founder of Ethical Culture) called leading congregants, all captains of industry, into his office, locked the door, announced the need, and let them go only when the project was funded. I've seen modern day member's of Adler's denomination lecture on their project in glowing terms without making an appeal, only to be interrupted by the most enthusiastic supporter waving a check – or hundred dollar bill. Then others are inspired to participate in like manner. Pentecostal Church of God section meetings may include an announcement of a need and various congregations vie for the honor of giving bigger, or proportionally bigger amounts. Bill Winston's congregants even bring money to place on the steps while he is preaching! Of course, you will select only those measures that seem ethical to you and to your congregation. I merely mean to point out that there are some creative methods.

There may be grants available. Ask your librarian where there is a library of granting agencies and respective interests. There is a library of granting agencies in Austin called The Hogg Library and there may be others around the nation. I expect that many more philanthropists would give to early childhood education were they to know about the magnitude of the need and the availability of reputable institutions meeting that need.

Please notice, however, that it is very rare for a grant to be made for a start-up. Normally a foundation or donor wants to be sure that 1) the people asking for money have already put their own money into the project, 2) the project is well run, and 3) is likely to have the desired outcome. Therefore, normally a center must be running three years with good financials and measurable achievements before it can obtain a grant. It always helps if the funding agency discovered that the requesting community has made its full effort. Often foundations want to fund expansions, never a start-ups and rarely ongoing budgets. However, seeing a stable, quality center, they should be persuaded that this is the high-benefit impact for their dollar. Scholarships, capital expansions, and especially equipment purchases, may be of interest to foundations. The best advice on writing grant application is to follow directions exactly.

When you are ready to consider your tuition model, first check in your neighborhood to find what is customary. Then consider sustainability both for the school and for families. I recommend charging some tuition, but not so high that most of the population cannot access your school. Here are some models.

- Low tuition across the board
- Full market tuition with some scholarships
- 2 tiers with a lower tuition for tithing congregants
- Sliding fee scale
- Some partial and some almost full scholarship
- Charter school: exchanging the religious words for free funding from the government

Then comes the question of how to award scholarships. You may have a committee sworn to secrecy, an outsourced company that keeps everyone's financial information confidential, or an unquestionably trusted benevolent dictator of clergy. Care must be taken in gathering pertinent information and structuring the committee.

You may wish to avoid having the director or pastor be official members of the committee. If you put this task on them, then there may be great personal pressure on them for favorable decisions; you might want to avoid this. If she or he is included, families may attempt to prevail on them for a good word, take up time, make trouble and possibly subvert the process. Relieve both directors and democratically elected pastors of these negative outcomes. Nevertheless, they have vital information without which your committee may stumble into disaster. Both director and pastor can and should confidentially advise without officially serving on the committee.

Not only keep both application information and committee decisions confidential but also obtain full information. Without full information, or you may find yourself subsidizing the wrong thing. Hard decisions must be made about what kinds of income to count and how to predict how money will be used and what children may profit the most. If you have an affluent student body and have only a few poorer students, be sure to give them enough so that they are not socially isolated within the school. If you have just two or three economic tiers within your student body, take care that this is not played out socially among the students.

Keeping up with the alumni you have helped in the past may be great encouragement to board, directors, teacher, and students. Ideally, some of your students will come back to be contributors. Many more wealthy schools use Grandparents' Day as an opportunity to do fundraising. If you have a school that is a charitable mission, then make a donors' day or make a tour of the school part of your regional missions fair. Don't forget to partner with other churches and agencies where appropriate. In all things, cultivate a Kingdom generosity. Showcasing your victories in students lives may help with these efforts.

10 LAST WORDS

A Few Warnings

Don't get yourself put in prison. In Texas, it is a **felony** to care for more than five children any of whom are not your own for more than four hours. Period. Well no, there are 2 exceptions. You may offer strictly religious instruction. That is why you don't need a license to have a Sunday School or a Catechism class. In Texas, similarly, you are able to provide a single focus activity. For instance, a karate dojo or an art studio may offer classes without a license. However, if you offer childcare, even just during the Superbowl, you need a license. Yes, there is a group that does this annually and got their license. Don't violate this.

Be precise in how your describe your center so that it is obvious that you are complying with the law. If you have a single focus program, do not claim to have an after-school center. Do not invite confusion or official investigation.

While I have taken some pains to set aside undue fear of authorities, I do not want anyone to become lax in complying with the law. Nor do I want imprecise wording to hurt you, the center, or your congregation.

You will not be permitted to spank children, threaten them with spanking or anything else, or even speak harshly to them. Even if it is legal in your state for parents to spank their own children, do not permit any spanking or any discussion of spanking at your licensed center. Even in Texas, a more conservative state than most, for decades the licensing and child protection authorities have had a policy that assumes any accusation of child abuse is true if religion is involved. In my high school Child Development class, the state Child Protective Services came to talk about their abuse hotline and what they did. The representative said that if the accusation of abuse includes mentioned that the accused is involved in religion, then the accusation was believed and acted upon immediately. So be sure you are clear on this. Even in 1972, if someone called on the abuse hotline and accused someone of abusing a child, if they also mentioned that the person in question was religious, then the state authorities, as a policy, believed the accusation and immediately removed the child from the family.

Today, most secular people think Christian education/rearing is primarily spanking -- and spanking is abuse. I realize that this train of thought is quite shocking to some church people. I remember when I tried to get advertising for my radio broadcast urging faith for healing of learning problems, including healthful lifestyle and innovative education practices, some shop owners would just not talk to me because they didn't want to be involved in promoting abuse! Clearly in their mind, no matter what I said, since I was a Christian talking about children on the air, I was promoting abuse. Incidentally, I never mentioned spanking. Only one guest even mentioned it in the 9 ½ years. (Dani Johnson, a mother of five, author and marketing trainer, did when she was my guest. She had no state issued educators credentials to protect. She is a millionaire mother on a crusade against pornography and for training children for life success.)

Given the licensing requirements, you will have to be not only compliant, but careful to avoid the hint of non-compliance. Even a church that strongly wishes to disagree should not risk harming the mission to outside children. Arguments, whether Biblical or scientific, may be made elsewhere, but for the well-being of the mission, one must comply with this law. Find other ways to help children make good choices and cultivate self-control.

Don't Underestimate the Role of the Director

Do not get a director who is inexperienced, a bad manager, or sloppy with the regulations. Most directors have come up from being a teacher, and while that is good, good management expertise is needed also. Often this is overlooked. For instance, there is a church not far from my home that no longer has a center and won't talk about one, because theirs was closed or threatened with closure. The root cause was that they hired from within, someone who was not qualified, and had a sloppy or overly carefree mentality. Then the center that didn't measure up to minimum standards. Now there is a sense of shame on the church leadership and more opportunities are being lost. It would be better to acknowledge the challenge to start with, and admit problems when they arrive, then fix them --- and continue to have the center.

Don't get a director who works against your vision. For instance, I know a center started by a foundation funded by a conservative evangelical. The vision document for the center said that the primary goal was conversions, character formation, and sending the children as a cohort to school. The thought was first to make an eternal improvement for the children, and then to make a better academic outcome than HeadStart obtains. It is known that gains made in HeadStart program evaporate out by sixth grade, if not earlier. It was a good vision. However, the foundation hired a religiously liberal director from a different denomination. She undoubtedly had the technical knowledge, but she had a contrary vision. She directly told me that she was not at all interested in conversions. She said that she felt that if she could just get the mothers reading to the children, then her aims would be met. Notice that while this might be a good aim, this was not in line with the published vision of the funder. I am not sure who hired her, or what her job description said, but I did detect a disconnect. Be sure your founding director aligns with your reasons for starting a center and with your vision for its aims.

I have known of numerous cases of the director being at odds with the pastor or board, for a wide variety of reasons. Most of these can be groups into three categories: 1) unclear organizational founding documents, 2) the church neglecting to pay attention so that over time a director began to believe the center was hers, and 3) the church abruptly and unreasonably interfering. Usually this interference is based on imaginary expertise and for its own monetary, and often only imagined, benefit. All of these could have been avoided. All of them waste time, energy, and effort.

Director Qualification Checklist

- Have a combination of formal education in early childhood and years of experience to meet state regulations. Note: without relevant formal education, you will not be able to obtain some accreditations, even if you are licensed. There are several Christian universities that offer Early Childhood studies.
- Ability to manage teachers and serve customers
- Ability to deal with or see that children who have problems are properly handled
- Ability to understand complex regulations and use good judgment
- Commitment to your vision and mission
- Ability to keep to the budget, do accounting, or work with those who do
- Ability to appropriately interact with board and church representatives

Most disaster stories start with inadequate structure, exacerbated by bad communication, with long neglect. Problems can be started or worsened by any of the parties involved. These are almost always remediable; the mission for the children need not be torpedoed. Often fixing the problem involves proper training of the board. Prevention is more pleasant than cure and much more pleasant than ongoing suffering. Setting things up clearly at first will prevent many problems. Personality clashes may be unavoidable, but are often only a quick explanation covering over a worrisome structural dynamic. In any case, proper recruiting, hiring, training, and casting a vision in line with mission vision is the answer – and getting professional organizational training and consulting when needed.

Don't Overlook the Importance of Having The Right Team

Good coaches spend real effort on recruiting. They don't accept just any player as long as they can pay minimum wage. The coach knows he needs the right players, deployed in the right way, paid well, and trained correctly. Only then will he have wins.

It would be lovely to think that you could hire from entirely from within in order to insure that your staff was in align with your doctrine and vision. While hiring from within is one of the secrets of congregationally affiliated centers, making for more stable and often more educated staff, it is seldom possible to hire ONLY from within. It is not reasonable to expect that you will have all the expertise you need in your own congregation. First, many members these days are surprisingly not in line with the doctrine of their church. Secondly, few churches have the needed expertise for a center entirely in their church. Expertise is very important. Doctrine is not as pertinent when we are talking about teaching preschoolers. Bible stories are pretty much the same for preschoolers whether they are told in a Roman Catholic or United Pentecostal Church – churches who could never interchange their high school faculties. Insist on both character and expertise. Stretch toward having a superior team. Look, instead, for people who have vision, expertise, can take direction from a director you can trust.

Of course, you do not want a situation in which all your staff is far away ideologically from your church's thought and community. I have seen this problem as much as I have seen centers run totally by the congregation's women without the needed competences in early childhood education or management. Don't disregard competing ideologies as mere trifles of youth or slogans of formal training. They make a difference. Insure your mission is met by gathering the right team.

You efforts at the outset are vital, but it is an ongoing process. Continue to manage the hiring process. Ensure training continues to reinforce your mission. Finally, of course, pray and stay in touch with God. God is your first resource, not your last resort.

CONCLUSION

Opening quality child development centers may be the most important mission for any congregation today. I hope I have helped you envision how you could make a difference in our world in a positive, substantial, and significant way. I hope I have allowed you to clearly see a new avenue for the Great Commission. Please review what you said your congregation's mission is. What are the needs? We all have a need to serve the Lord. Most of us believe that forming a relationship with the eternal God through faith, based on divine grace, has eternal, everlasting consequences. The children have a need to be formed into Godly character because only that will allow them to have a good life. Only that will allow us to have a good society. Even if your congregation is highly invested in home education and parental responsibility, if you can stretch to take care of the children who are not taken care of, you have made a great missionary endeavor. Children in Africa are hearing the gospel; children in rural India and Yemen are beginning to hear the gospel; but increasingly children in the United States are not. Can you serve them?

Yes, there are real obstacles. I hope I have laid them out clearly so you can address them. I hope I have shown you that the obstacles can be overcome. You now have checklists to map what must be done. With patience and effort, you can get through each step. The difficult investment of the initial setup will pay large, ongoing dividends. Think of the center open. Think of children coming every day. It's like church five times a week! More teachers. More pupils. More learning. More caring. Think of the single mothers who are relieved from worry about their children. Then think of rank upon rank of adults who were once children in your church's CDC. Think of the leaders of the future who were formed in your center. That is a priceless treasure you have given to the world.

Surely you will invest now? Will you start going through the checklists? Will you start talking it up among your people? Will you lead them to lead in this most important of all missions?

Will you call me if you need help?

Let's partner for expansion of the Kingdom of God. Let's go into all the world, starting with your neighborhood. Let's share good news with them before it gets any worse for them. Imagine how you will feel at the end of time, when you look back on your ministry and legacy. How many people will you have formed in the Christian faith and discipleship? How many leaders? How many from them? Start today with expansion of the Kingdom of God through starting a Christian child development center and take care of children whom no one else is taking care of.

Grace and peace,

Sharon Sarles www.orgstrat.net 512-249-7629 desk phone

OFFERS

I do consult. Call me now 512/249-7629.

I am developing a course. Look for information at www.teachachildchangeanation.org or write to P.O. Box 971 Cedar Park, Texas 78630

I do offer training for small business, congregations/small denominations, and especially for child development centers. For more information, please go to www.orgstrat.net.

There are training materials available via CD and online for CDC directors and staff. I do have a binder for the use of center Directors, that contains training for the first 8 hours a new hire must have before joining a staff. It consists of the 8 hours required in Texas, on the topic required, in audio format on CDs, with reproducible paper and pencils tests.

I also will offer a plan for after-school centers, in a binder. Please inquire.

I hope to shortly begin to offer conferences for pastors and Christian directors. Please send me your email if you want to have announcements from this mission.

Whatever you do, please act today. Start. Souls, your budget, your legacy, your neighborhood, and many children depend upon it.

DECISIONS:

What is my congregation's most important mission? How does a CDC fit in with that mission?

How adequate is the building? What steps might be needed to make is adequate for a CDC?

What number of children might we help?

Make a rough/tentative vision budget.

What specific things do I still need to know?

Who can I contact to find out these things?

TO DO LIST:

TIMELINE:

TO STOP DOING LIST:

WHO YOU NEED TO CONTACT TO HELP YOU:

REFERENCES

After School Alliance. 2007. Afterschool Programs: Keeping Kids — and Communities Safe. *After School Alert Issue Brief.* April. http://www.afterschoolalliance.org/issue_briefs/issue_CrimeI B_27.pdf.

Allen, S & Daly, K. 2007. *The Effects of Father Involvement: Updated Research Summary of the Evidence.* Father Involvement Research Alliance. http://www.fira.ca/cms/documents/29/Effects_of_Father_Invo lvement.pdf.

Barna Research. 2016. "Five Trends Among the Unchurched." *Research Releases in Culture and Media*, Oct. 9, 2014, https://www.barna.org/barna-update/culture/685-five-trends-among-the-unchurched#.VtCKbkAeqSc (Accessed March 2, 2016).

Bidwell, Allie. 2013. American Students Fall in International Academic Tests, Chinese Lead the Pack. U.S. News and World Report, Dec. 3. https://www.usnews.com/news/articles/2013/12/03/american-students-fall-in-international-academic-tests-chinese-lead-the-pack.

Center for Disease Control. 2017. National Statistics: Unmarried Childbearing. https://www.cdc.gov/nchs/fastats/unmarried-childbearing.htm.

Child Protective Service of Texas, representative in Child Development Class, Bellaire High School, Bellaire, Texas. Spring 1972.

Children-and-Divorce.com. 2017. https://www.children-and-divorce.com/children-divorce-statistics.html.

Coleman, James S. 1988. "Social Capital" and schools: One reason for higher private school achievement. *Education Digest*, 53, 6-9.

Coleman J. S. 1986. *Individual Interests and Collective Action: Selected essays,* Cambridge Univ. Pr.

Coleman, J.S. 1982. *High School Acheivement: Public, Catholic, and private schools compared.* NY: Basic Books.

Dana Center. 2000. *Equity-Driven Achievement-Focused School Districts: Report on Systemic School Success in Four Texas School Districts Serving Diverse Student Populations.* The University of Texas, September. http://www.utdanacenter.org/downloads/products/equitydistricts.pdf.

DeSilver, D. 2017. "U.S. Student Achievement Still Lags Behind that of their Peers in Many Other Countries. Pew Research Center. February 15. http://www.pewresearch.org/fact-tan.

Editorial Projects in Education Research Center. (2004, August 3). Issues A-Z: After-School Programs. *Education Week.* Retrieved Month Day, Year from http://www.edweek.org/ew/issues/after-school-programs/ k/2017/02/15/u-s-students-internationally-math-science/.

Dunckley, Victoria. 2013. Nature's RX: Green Time's Affect on ADHD. *Psychology Today*, June 20. **https://www.psychologytoday.com/blog/mental-wealth/201306/natures-rx-green-times-effects-adhd**.

Fidellow, Barbara. 2017. Personal Report. San Antonio, January.

Gross, D. "'Porn-Key' Kids, " *XXX Church.* https://www.xxxchurch.com/thehaps/porn-key-kids.html.

Hymowitz, H. 2012. 'The Real, Complex Connection Between Single-Parent Families and Crime.' *The Atlantic*. Dec. 3. https://www.theatlantic.com/sexes/archive/2012/12/the-real-complex-connection-between-single-parent-families-and-crime/265860/.

Iserbyt, C.T. 1999. *The Deliberate Dumbing Down of America - A Chronological Paper Trail,* (C. Weatherly, ed.). Ravenna, OH, Conscience Press.

Jacobson, L. 2013. *CNN"s Don Lemon Says More than 72% of African American Births are Out of Wedlock*. July 29. http://www.politifact.com/truth-o-meter/statements/2013/jul/29/don-lemon/cnns-don-lemon-says-more-72-percent-african-americ/.

Jiung, Yang. 2017. *Basic Facts About Low Income Children: Children Under 3 2015*. National Center for Child Poverty. January. http://www.nccp.org/publications/pub_1171.html.

Jeynes, W. 2003. *Religion, Education, and Academic Success.* Greenwich, CN: IAP.

Lips, D. & Mulhausen, D. 2010. *Head Start Earns an F: No Lasting Impact by First Grade*. The Heritage Foundation. January 21. http://www.heritage.org/education/report/head-start-earns-f-no-lasting-impact-children-first-grade.

McLanahan, S., Tach, L., and Schneider, D. 2013. *The Causal Effects of Father Absence.* Annu Rev Sociol. 2013 Jul; 39: 399–427. doi: 10.1146/annurev-soc-071312-145704.

Montessori, Maria. 1965. *The Child in the Church*. St. Paul: Catechetical Guild.

---- 1965. *Spontaneous Activity in Education*. NY: Schocken.

National Center for Child Poverty. 2017. *Child Poverty*.
http://www.nccp.org/topics/childpoverty.html.

National Center for Fathering. 2017. *The Extent of Fatherlessness*.
http://www.fathers.com/statistics-and-research/the-extent-of-fatherlessness/.

OJJDP (Office of Juvenile Justice of the US Dept. of Justice) 2014
Statistical Briefing Book. May 22.
http://www.ojjdp.gov/ojstatbb/offenders/qa03401.asp?qaDate=2010.

---- Violent Crime Victimization 2014. Victimization for 1,000
Juvenile victims within age groups 1-11 and 12-17.
https://www.ojjdp.gov/ojstatbb/victims/qa02804.asp?qaDate=2014.

Pederson, J., de Kanter, A., Bobo, L.,Weinig, K., Noeth, K. 1999.
Safe and Smart: Making the After-School Hours Work for Kids, December 29. Document No.: 179991
https://www.ncjrs.gov/pdffiles1/nij/grants/179991.pdf.

Pew Research Center. 2015. *Parenting in America*. Dec. 15.
http://www.pewsocialtrends.org/2015/12/17/1-the-american-family-today/.

Popham, W. James. 2001. *The Truth about Testing: An Educator's Call to Action*. Alexandria, VA: Association for Supervision and Curriculum Development.

U.S. Census Bureau. 2016. *The Majority of Children Live with Two Parents,* Census Bureau Reports, Release Number:
CB16-192, Nov. 17, https://www.census.gov/newsroom/press-releases/2016/cb16-192.html.

U.S. Dept. of Health and Human Services. 2010. *Head Start Research*.
https://www.acf.hhs.gov/sites/default/files/opre/hs_impact_study_final.pdf.

Vespa, J., Lewis, J.M., and Kreider, R. 2013. *America's Family Living Arrangements 2012: Population Characteristics*. U.S. Census Bureau August 2013. https://www.census.gov/prod/2013pubs/p20-570.pdf.

Youth.gov [2017] *Afterschoolprograms*. https://youth.gov/youth-topics/afterschool-programs.

ABOUT THE AUTHOR

Sharon Sarles served the church from a young age, eventually as a growth pastor, and then went on to be a college instructor, broadcaster and writer. She served as a turn-around agent for a church affiliated preschool. Currently a trainer, coach, and business consultant for childcare directors and owners.

Made in the USA
Las Vegas, NV
02 September 2021

29490978R00059